GOING SANE
SERIES

****

Heroes
Of The
Heart

Treasured Stories Of
Hurt, Hate, Horror
And
HUMOR

*****

Don Doyle, DMin, PhD

****

Asa HOUSE Books
Memphis, TN 1995

Going Sane
Series

Heroes of the Heart

by
Don Doyle, DMin, PhD

Published by:

Asa HOUSE Books
P.O. Box 381604
Memphis, TN 38183
901/ 751-4140

Copyright @ 1995
First Printing 1995

Library of Congress Catalog Number 95-71707

Doyle, Don
ISBN   1-57087-200-7
162 Pages
$17.95

About the Author

Since 1966, Dr. Don Doyle has functioned in some official capacity as a minister, counselor, or psychotherapist. In that period of time, he has logged more than 32,000 hours of listening to people from 42 states and 18 foreign countries.

With degrees in biology, theology, and marriage and family counseling, Dr. Doyle brings a varied background to the counseling room. A former pastor for twelve years, he also served for three years as a naval aviation officer.

For eight years, Dr. Doyle was Associate Director of the *Burlingame Counseling Center*, in Burlingame, California. Since 1987, he has directed the *Doyle Family Counseling Center* in Memphis, Tennessee.

For information or consultation, write or call:

Dr. Don Doyle
2606 Maple Grove Cove N.
Germantown, TN 38139
901/757-2347

Acknowledgments

Deep gratitude is expressed to all who contributed time and energy in helping bring this project to fruition. Their assistance with proofing and editing was invaluable. To name any is to miss some. However, at the risk of doing that, I would like to express my appreciation to the following: Judy Birchler, Mike and Michaelle Davis, Maggie Haas, Janet Jackson, Missy Martin, Joan Moore, Bill and Eliza Shields, Lois Varney.

In addition, I'd like to thank my family: Matt and Wende Doyle, Leanne and Kelly Duncan, Chad Doyle, and my wife, Martha. All of them graciously tolerated many months of incessant conversations about "The Book."

Special thanks to: Roe Kienle for the excellent artistic illustrations; Jann Sessoms for tireless efforts in editing; and Wende Doyle for the great job with the jacket cover design.

Preface

The GOING SANE SERIES is about life, living, and the pursuit of happiness. It's about people. Real people. It's about their successes and failures in finding contentment in life.

I've been listening to people for a long time. All my life, I suppose. Since 1966, I've functioned in some formal capacity as a *listener*. In that period of time, I've heard a lot of narratives. Heroes of the Heart is a composite of essays and short stories about some of these experiences, and some of these people. It's about what I have observed, and what I think I've learned along the way.

Some of these pieces will make you laugh. Others may bring some tears. One or two of my conclusions may be controversial enough to provoke some anger. Hopefully, a few will make you think. My desire is that in every chapter you will find at least a trace of inspiration to make your day better.

To have been included in the lives of those who have shared with me is a sacred treasure. To pass these experiences along is intended to honor them.

Heroes of the Heart was chosen as the title to reflect my deep admiration and affection for those who have told me their stories. They really are my *heroes*.

Virtually all the stories are paradoxical. While

having a simple plot, they reveal some of the most complicated human issues. In spite of seeming elementary, they represent the complexity and enormity of human suffering.

All the stories are true. All the people are real. However, the names and the locations are totally fictitious (except when specified). Any resemblance to anyone you know is purely coincidental.

This book was written as a dialogue with each reader. Therefore, the writing style is strictly conversational.

Contents

1. Never Play Leapfrog With a Unicorn   13

2. Cleaning Up the Mess   19

3. Finding the Missing Peace   25

4. A Con Man to the Core   31

5. Riding the Tiger   35

6. Divorced Forever   41

7. Hold Off on Buying the Rope   45

8. Some Things You Miss, You Miss Forever   49

9. Unsensible Blame   55

10. The Marriage Wheel   59

11. "Don't I Know You?"   65

12. Just Relax   71

13. Can You Trust Feelings?   77

14. Easy on the Eyes   85

15. "Whachuruninfrum?"   89

16. The Big Mac Attack   95

17. Chip Off the Old Block?   103

18. Bad Goodbyes   109

19. Boogie-Woogie on Beale Street   113

20. "I'm Not Very Good at Feeling Bad"   121

21. "It Was Them Navel Oranges"   129

22. Wasted Worry   133

23. The Folly of Fanaticism   139

24. The Accidental Tourist   143

25. Beginnings and Endings   149

Introduction

In its best form, psychotherapy is about spiritual and emotional growth through self-discovery. In fact, a literal translation of psyche and therapy is "healing of the soul." It is my hope that this book will assist you in accomplishing that task.

Since journaling is one of the most effective tools in the therapeutic process, I have designed this book accordingly. Having personally and professionally used journaling for more than twenty-five years, I strongly recommend it as a tool for spiritual and emotional growth.

Those in therapy who journal consistently make progress much more rapidly than those who don't.

Just reading this book can and will be therapeutic. However, doing the suggested journaling after reading each chapter, will tremendously increase its effectiveness and value.

While you are reading, pretend that you are sitting in a group therapy session. Envision that a group member or the group leader is sharing the information or story with you. As much as possible, let yourself "be there" to experience your responses and reactions. As the sharing is taking place, listen to your head and heart.

When you finish the chapter, in your journal, answer these four questions:

1. What thoughts did you have?

2. What feelings did you experience?

3. What memories came up for you?

4. What insights did you gain as a result of this exercise?

To achieve maximum benefit, after reading each chapter, answer these four questions before going to the next chapter.

At another time, you can use what you have written as a catalyst for some in-depth journaling.

Dedicated

To

Martha

Whose harassment made me start it;
Whose patience let me finish it;
Whose love made it all worthwhile.

Chapter 1

Never Play Leapfrog
With A Unicorn

Jayne was a member of **MENSA**. She told me so in the first few moments of our conversation. Wanting to be sure that I knew about **MENSA**, she said: "That's the organization for those whose IQ is in the top 2 percent."

I said, "I'm a member of **DENSA** myself."

"What's that?" she asked. "I've never heard of DENSA."

"That's the organization for dense people who are in the other 98 percent," I said, smiling.

She didn't smile back. Clearly, she wasn't sure someone from MENSA could be helped by someone from DENSA.

Knowing I was losing ground, I forged on. This was her first therapy session so I suggested she tell me why she was seeking my help.

Her story? She was forty-three, had been married and divorced twice. She dated men twenty years younger, and couldn't understand why they dropped her. She dated married men, and couldn't understand why they wouldn't marry her. She picked up men at bars, and was afraid she might have AIDS. She couldn't understand why her grown children didn't show her more respect.

Jayne withdrew from law school after one semester. She didn't like their philosophy. She took an art course, but quit after six weeks. They squashed her creativity. She'd rejected medical school because of their rigidity. She worked in the corporate world for six years, and had quit or been fired from six different jobs.

She hated her mother but went to visit every weekend. She loved her father but he was dead. She was overweight. She obsessed about it. But it didn't keep her from eating Oreos, Twinkies, and loads of chocolate.

In the past year, Jayne had been cited for DUI twice, which made her third offense. Her driver's license had been revoked. She continued to drive.

After telling her story through a maze of sobs, she said: "If I'm so smart, why is my life in such chaos?"

Good question. I wasn't sure she wanted the answer. At least, not all at once. So, with a little humor, I watered it down a bit.

"Your life is in chaos because you've consistently broken one of life's basic commandments: *Never Play Leapfrog With a Unicorn.*"

Smiling for the first time, she said weakley, "What does that mean?"

I said, "We DENSA folks have to make things simple. We don't have as many options as you MENSA people. We have limitations, and we must have some boundaries."

"So, we subscribe to a few rules and we try to exercise the discipline to follow them. One of those rules is *Never Play Leapfrog With a* Unicorn--

because that's just plain dumb. No matter how smart you are, eventually you'll end up with a horn in your rear."

"Jayne, that's the reason your life is in a mess. You've been doing some really dumb things for too many years."

"Can you help me?" she asked.

My response was, "Yes, I can, provided you're willing to do two things. *First*, you'll deal with the cause of the problem, rather than the symptom. *Second*, you'll learn some new habits for your life." And she did.

Sometimes it's hard to decide whether highly intelligent people are blessed or cursed. From childhood days, they were indoctrinated with dramatic and excessive superlatives, such as:

"There's nothing you can't do." "You're the smartest student in this school." "You can figure out anything." "You're brilliant." "You're a genius."

They are inundated with high expectations. Often, they've been programmed to deny their limitations. They have no boundaries, and very little discipline.

It's also true that moderately intelligent children are frequently programmed the same way. If all the children were brilliant, whose parents believed and told them they were brilliant, this would be a world full of brilliant people.

However, it really doesn't matter. Whether you're in the upper 2 percent, or the lower 98 percent, you do have limitations. Without boundaries that are clear, and discipline that you live by, there's a good chance you'll find yourself in a quandary-- the same as when you play leapfrog with a unicorn.

Chapter 2

Cleaning Up The Mess

Like countless others, after seeing <u>A River Runs Through It</u>, I was smitten with the fly fishing bug. (Since that movie, I understand that sales of fly fishing equipment have skyrocketed.)

From the opening monologue of Norman Maclean's marvelous story, I was hooked.

****

In our family there was no clear line between religion and fly fishing. We lived at the junction of great trout rivers in western Montana, and our father was a Presbyterian minister and a fly fisherman who tied his own flies and taught others. He told us about Christ's disciples being fishermen, and we were left to assume, as my brother and I did, that all first class fishermen on the Sea of Galilee were fly fishermen and that John, the favorite, was a dry-fly fisherman.

*****

With visions of catching big cutthroat trout, to celebrate my youngest son Chad's twenty-first birthday, we went to Montana to fly fish. We toured Yellowstone Park. Rode horses in the high country. We enjoyed some great fishing, and met an extraordinary man.

His name is Max Chase. He owns the *Point of Rocks Guest Ranch* at Emigrant Gap, Montana. He's been leading hunting parties and fly fishing trips for thirty years. A few years back, he was the Montana fly fishing champion. He's independent, opinionated, and a good businessman. He was our host and fishing guide on the Yellowstone River.

One afternoon, while in some swift current, Chad saw an aluminum can in the edge of the water and pointed it out.

Max Chase, with a few choice words, began rowing against the current with all his might. He was determined to retrieve that *intolerable intruder*. After ten to fifteen minutes, he finally accomplished the mission. With me holding a willow limb, and Max using the oars, Chad got into the water. In a few moments, he plucked that eyesore from the cold, clear waters of the Yellowstone River.

With the trash in hand, we were all cheering and laughing. After a couple of minutes, I said, "Max, was it worth it?" He laughed and said, "Oh yeah, definitely!"

After he used a few more choice words about people that trash and pollute, we resumed our fishing.

Oh, I forgot to tell you. Max Chase loves life, liberty, family, and *mother earth*. He loves these things enough that he's willing to clean up someone else's mess. Maybe that's the acid test of true love. Perhaps that's the heart of *agape-love*-- to will the highest good to all of creation.

Regarding environmental issues, another story reveals a sharp contrast in attitudes and action.

Carl was an avid environmentalist. Several years ago, he did some intensive therapy with me. He belonged to several ecology organizations. Over the years, he had contributed to congressional lobbyists who were trying to get legislation passed regarding the environment. He obsessed about trash and clutter. He complained and criticized. He confronted litter bugs. He was angry about the way people polluted and desecrated the good earth. He worried about the future conditions of the air, land, and streams which his grandkids would inherit.

His concern was commendable, but I was bothered by something about his anger. One day, I said, "I've been listening to your hostility about trash and pollution, and I'm curious about something. I know you don't litter, but do you pick up what other people have thrown out?"

"Absolutely not!" he said with indignation. "I'm not cleaning up somebody else's mess!"

I went on. "Does that mean if you saw a stryrofoam cup in the parking lot, you'd step over it, rather than pick it up?"

"Absolutely!" he said, again. This time with stronger irritation.

I replied, "With an attitude like that, the environmental problem will never be solved. Until enough people care enough to clean up somebody else's mess, our environment will continue to deteriorate."

I believe this is a truth that applies to every aspect of life. Most of the people who get into therapy are learning to clean up the mess someone else made in their lives. Until they stop being angry and blaming others, nothing ever really changes. It's true for individuals, and it's true for the masses.

Caring enough to clean up somebody else's mess is what changes the world. It's hard work. You may say a few choice words along the way. But it's definitely worth it.

Thanks, Max Chase, for validating my belief.

Chapter 3

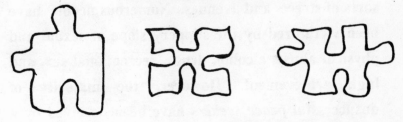

Finding The Missing

Peace

"**W**hat's the biggest problem that causes people to get into therapy?"

That's a question I've been asked numerous times. Sometimes, it's asked by those who are considering therapy for themselves. Periodically, it comes from those in therapy who want assurance that their problems are not unique. On some occasions, it's raised by those who are just curious.

Okay, what's the answer? Why do people get into therapy? Because they're trying to find *peace of mind*. They may not call it that, but that's what they want. It's an elusive search and leads through all sorts of streets and avenues. Numerous people have been victimized by the slippery slope of sexual and physical abuse, alcohol, drugs, recreational sex, and high achievement. However, the majority of unsuccessful *peace seekers* have been deceived by a widespread false premise-- *that every dilemma has a solution-- that every situation in life is either good or bad, right or wrong, black or white.*

My sister, Sheila, has taught kindergarten for more than twenty-five years. Over that period, she's collected a lot of stories. One gem involved a youngster who was obviously a victim of the "every problem has a solution" syndrome. During recess, the class had been outside in the August heat. After a few minutes, the little guy approached my sister and lamented, "Ms. Kirkpatrick, I've got on sunblock, but I'm still hot!"

In some form or fashion, all of us have been told that every problem has a resolution, and every question has an answer. The truth about life (as I have seen it and experienced it) is not so simple.

At the core of human existence, there is *ambiguity about what we know, ambivalence about how we feel, and anxiety about who we are.*

We don't really know very much, for certain. Our feelings are usually mixed. And we're always a little uneasy about who we are. That's the way life really is. Those are the hard facts about the human condition. That's what theologians call finitude-- the distinct limitations of being human.

We tend to reject this truth because it's not the way we want it to be. But when we are honest and open blind eyes, that's what we discover. *Life is mystery.*

That's scary. Discovering and embracing this reality gives credence to the maxim: "The truth will set you free-- but first it will make you miserable!"

Fearing the misery, many people refuse to embrace the mystery. So, they create absolutes to counter the human condition. Absolutes in education, politics, religion. They put blinders on and live in denial with a phoney set of absolutes. But nothing really changes; life at its core is still mystery.

Many years ago, I helped conduct a funeral, along with Elder Van Maxwell, a South Georgia, country preacher. Reverend Maxwell was the keynote speaker. I read scripture, said a prayer, and sat down.

Mr. Maxwell was a seasoned veteran at conducting funerals. Very slowly, he stepped up to the lectern. I'll never forget his opening line, because every word was spoken deliberately and convincingly: "Every time I stand in the presence of death, my feelings are always the same-- mystery and fear."

I do not remember what he said after that. That was enough. I do remember thinking that Elder Van Maxwell was speaking for us all. In the face of death, mystery and fear abound. I believe that's true, not only when we stare into the face of death, but also, when we honestly face life. Life is filled with ambiguity, ambivalence, and anxiety.   Absolutes emerge to counter   reality.

In my opinion, peace of mind comes not from subscribing to absolutes, but from learning to make adjustments. *Every problem does not have an answer, but every dilemma does require an adjustment.*

Trying to find peace of mind is like climbing a slippery slope that is slick with mystery and fear. Peace of mind comes to those who find enough grace to come to grips with the adjustments that must be made, and keep moving forward.

Beloved professor, theologian, and scholar, Dale Moody, referred to the spiritual experience as a "leap of faith." What he meant was-- you can never know for sure. You can never have all the answers before or after you act. You just make your choice and take the leap.

Regarding most aspects of living, "the leap of faith" is a great metaphor. Amidst the ambiguity, ambivalence, and anxiety, well-integrated people learn to act. They celebrate their successes, learn from their mistakes, grieve about their losses, and take the next leap.

There's an ancient proverb that says, "Leap and the net will appear." I would add, "sometimes." Sometimes the net appears, and sometimes you fall on your face. Well-adjusted people (just as the words imply) make adjustments to life as it is, and continue leaping, anyway.

Making adjustments to life's demands and continuing to leap is the truth that is beautifully portrayed throughout the Academy Award winning Driving Miss Daisy. Toward the end of the movie, two scenes particularly emphasized this point.

In the first, Hoke returns to the house where he had served as Miss Daisy's chauffeur. The house is empty. Miss Daisy is in the nursing home. In the front yard is a *For Sale* sign.

Reminiscing as he walked through the house, Hoke surprisingly finds Boolie, Miss Daisy's son. They spend a few minutes talking about the changing times.

Inquiring about his old friend, Hoke asks, "Mr. Werthan, how's Miss Daisy doing?"

"Hoke, she has her good days and her bad days," Boolie reckons.

Hoke nods, "Yesah, don't we all!"

I suspect he's right. That's the way life is for all, young or old, rich or poor-- good days and bad days.

In the second scene, Hoke visits Miss Daisy in the nursing home.   They have a warm nostalgic reunion.

"How're you doing, Hoke?" she asks.

Hoke responds. "Well, Miss Daisy, I'm just doing the best I can."

Nodding her head with understanding, Miss Daisy says, "Me too, Hoke."

Hoke's eyes just twinkle, when he replies, "Yesam. I reckon that's about all there is to it!" Both nod and chuckle.

In the good days and bad days, just doing the best you can.   Taking life as it comes-- refusing to buy the false premise that every problem has a solution. Embracing the mystery of life, and having enough grace to adjust to it. Maybe that really is about all there is to it.

Isn't that what finding the missing peace is all about? I think it is.

Chapter 4

A Con Man To
The Core

Bill's whole life had been a lie. He had cheated in business. Swindled money. Defrauded the government. Hoodwinked his way through college and law school.

After many years of living a lie, he decided to do some intensive therapy. Finally, he would turn his life around. He wanted to repent, wipe the slate clean, and get a fresh start.

Coming from Iowa, Bill was scheduled for a three-week intensive. During his first session, Bill was told: *The truth will set you free, but first it will make you miserable*.

From that very first session, he said he was ready for the pain. He was going to tell the whole truth, and nothing but the truth. He unraveled his story. It was quite a tale. The center piece of his lifetime of scam occurred in law school.

Bill had a speech impediment. Wondering how long he had stammered, a fellow student asked him about the problem.

Bill responded, "Since I was in Vietnam. I crashed an F4 Phantom in the Gulf of Tonkin. My co-pilot got tangled up in his parachute. I could see he was in trouble. I swam to him. Tried to rescue him, but I didn't make it. He went under just a few feet from my outstretched fingers. I was screaming for him to hang on. He drowned. I've been stuttering ever since."

"My God in heaven!" said his listener, tears streaming down his face. "That's the most horrible story I've ever heard. You're a real survivor. You're a great role model."

The listener and newly converted "Fan of Bill" turned and called for two other friends to come hear this terrible story.

The second time he told it, Bill was even better. More convincing. More dramatic. More emotional. This time he spiced it up with more gory details.

Word spread around campus. He became known as a war hero— a naval aviator, traumatized over the death of his friend, left with a speech impediment. Everyone knew the story by heart.

At the end of his second year, he was recruited to run for president of the student body. On the *War Hero Ticket,* he won by a landslide.

During the first week of his third and final year, Bill was having a beer with some classmates. Someone said, "Hey Bill, come over and meet this new transfer student. You guys have a lot in common. He's an ex-naval aviator. Flew F4's, just like you."

Uh, oh. A few minutes later, the jig was up. The new student turned from Bill and said to the others, "I'm not sure what's going on here. I don't know who this guy is, but he's never flown an F4. He's never even been in one!"

For his unethical conduct, Bill was suspended from law school for one year. After the suspension, he was allowed to return and finish his studies.

During his therapy, Bill sobbed his heart out. Agonized over this shameful scam. In addition, he told dozens of similar stories. He had cheated on his wives, gypped his partners, and swindled money from clients. He dumped out his agony and torment due to habitual lying.

Over a three-week period, Bill worked with four different therapists. All of us who worked with him, also wept with him. Seldom had we seen such a determined effort to break a lifetime of compulsivity.

Bill wanted to stay longer. He was finally getting well. He didn't want to quit before he was finished.

To make the space for him, all of us canceled appointments and rearranged our schedules. We worked out a fourth week for him. Anyone so determined, deserved our best efforts.

On his final day, the entire staff, including office workers and therapists, had a little farewell party. There were lots of tears, hugs, and "thank yous." It was a great day for all of us.

****

EPILOGUE. Bill paid for his therapy with a check. It bounced. The address he had given was phoney. We never saw or heard from Bogus Bill again.

MORAL. If you're doing therapy with a con man, make sure he pays up front!

Chapter 5

Riding The Tiger

The ancient proverb says, "Man who decides to ride tiger shows sign of great courage. But same man shows sign of great wisdom if he decides well in advance how he plans to dismount."

For nearly thirty years, I've listened to numerous stories of dissatisfaction related to work, career, and profession.

"If I had it to do over, I'd do something different," is a common statement. It's been said by doctors, lawyers, teachers, journalists, business men/women, nurses,   accountants,   factory workers,

Having mounted the tiger, without a plan for dismounting, they assume they just have to keep riding. They stay mounted, long after the painful discovery that their work is unfulfilling. Sometimes it's boring and far from being what they really want to do.

When our oldest son, Matt, was about fourteen, he made an interesting observation concerning work. He was lamenting that he needed more money. Being given an allowance for doing household chores wasn't enough. He surmised that things would be better if he had more income.

Responding to his dilemma, I said, "Son, have you considered getting a job?"

I'll never forget his answer.

"Well, Dad, I would get a job. But once you start working, you don't ever get to stop. You always say that you've been working all your life. I know I'll have to start working pretty soon, but I'd like to postpone it as long as possible."

To be totally candid, I thought he had a pretty good point. And I told him. My position may not be completely consistent with what Matt surmised, but it's pretty close.

My assessment: Life is too short, and too much of it is spent doing what we call work, not to enjoy and experience fulfillment from it.

As Kemmons Wilson, founder of Holiday Inn, put it, "To be successful in life, you only have to work half-a-day, and it doesn't matter which twelve hours you pick!"

In the same speech, delivered to a group of teenagers, Mr. Wilson said, "Find a job that you love, and you'll never have to work a day in your life."

When people decide to be honest with themselves, and decide to pursue their *inner calling*, remarkable changes occur in lives and careers.

It's been a pleasure to watch many people come to grips with *who they really are*, rather than continue riding a tiger that didn't fit. I've known some men and women who made some radical changes.

Examples: I know a physician who became an archaeologist, a housewife who's now a lawyer, an engineer who became a house husband, an accountant who is now a psychotherapist. I know a computer engineer who is now a composer, and a minister who became a florist. I know a teacher who turned to nursing, a corporate executive who entered the ministry. And dozens of other equally surprising career changes. Each of them decided it was time to get off the tiger.

Some people stay on their *career tiger* thinking

they're too old to change. A man said to me, "If I was younger, I'd become a lawyer. But I'd have to go back to college for a year or two and then three years of law school. It'd take me five years, and I'd be forty-five by then."

I said, "If you don't pursue that goal, how old will you be in five years?"

Many got on their *career tiger* when they were very young. The proverbial, "What do you want to be when you grow up?" is something we all remember. Choosing a career at such an early age is one of the strangest aspects of modern life.

When our daughter, Leanne, was in the middle of her freshman year in college, she called home on a Wednesday night. Said she was coming home for the weekend. She wanted to be sure that I would have ample time to do some "...serious talking." When I asked what was pressing her, she said, "I have to decide what I'm going to do with the rest of my life!"

Startled, I said, "By this weekend?!"

Such an experience is not unique. Almost all parents and students have had similar experiences.

Our educational system expects students to choose a *major* when they enroll in college. Making such a significant decision at such an early age is frequently irrational. Often the choice is highly influenced by parents or teachers. Repeatedly, it leads toward much frustration and pain.

Louise was an interesting person. She was an R.N. and had a teaching credential. In telling her story, she related, "I only lasted one semester in a classroom. Then I quit and went to nursing school."

As Louise continued sharing her history, she said, "From the first day, I hated teaching. I hung on till the term ended. Thought I could last the whole year. By Thanksgiving, I knew I'd be lucky if I made it till Christmas."

I asked Louise how she decided to become a teacher. I'll never forget her answer. It was one of the strangest things I've ever heard.

"The day I registered for classes as a beginning freshman, I was shocked by the long registration lines. So, I looked around until I found the shortest line. At that point, the only short line was in the education department. So, that's what I picked."

This story sounds ludicrous. But it may reflect more reality than we're willing to admit. Quite obviously, numerous careers are chosen *accidentally* more than *intentionally*.

Perhaps that's what Thoreau was reacting to when he left society and went into the woods to live in seclusion. To explain his actions, he said:

****

> I went to the woods because I chose to live deliberately. To confront the essentials of life. To see if I could learn what it had to teach. Rather than come to die, and discover that I had not lived.

****

I don't know how you got on your tiger. However, if you're tired of riding it, maybe it's time to get some help with a plan for dismounting.

Chapter 6

Divorced Forever

"You'll be divorced forever." That's a statement I make to couples with children who are contemplating divorce or have already terminated. It's my way of emphasizing the obvious, but often overlooked reality.

Two people who have *parented* together will always have a relationship. Divorce does not solve the relational problem, just alters it. It may be a divorced relationship, rather than a married relationship. Nonetheless, those who have parented together will be in some form of relationship forever.

A divorced couple with children will be thrown together on special occasions such as graduations, sporting events, music recitals, weddings, and family deaths. And then comes the birth of grandchildren. These experiences will go on for the remainder of their lives.

Couples who leave a relationship in hostility and bitterness often continue in the same manner. Those who do not resolve this conflict continue to have those feelings activated again and again. The course of normal events, which include their children, repeatedly bring the divorced couple into the same arena.

The stories I could tell (and no doubt the stories you know about or have experienced) verify my claim. Some couples who have been divorced for ten, fifteen, or twenty years still cannot converse in a rational manner. They cannot attend a common function, or in some cases, be in the same room together without being inundated with resentment or remorse.

Quite often, family members will cooperate with this neurotic behavior, and frequently are forced to take sides. It's common to hear:

"Well, you know how Mom is, she won't come if Dad is going to be there."

"We'll have to get with Dad another time, he's still too bitter at Mom to be around her."

"If Mom knew I was going to see Dad, she'd be devastated."

"If Dad knew I was taking Mom on vacation, he'd be enraged."

How absurd and ridiculous. Two adults, who had a bad marriage, continue the pattern by having a bad divorce. In so doing, everyone around them is uncomfortable. Sometimes miserable. What a waste of energy.

I've heard many people say they wished their ex-spouses were dead. This meant they wouldn't be subjected to having contact with him or her ever again. Meaning, of course, that death of the ex-spouse would relieve them of their unwanted feelings. Such an attitude puts the emphasis in the wrong place.

Your feelings are yours; and yours to deal with. You have no right to make your ex-spouse responsible for your feelings. Take charge of your life. Refuse to live in the past. Choose to have a healthy divorce. Otherwise, a lasting peace of mind will be an illusion.

Divorced couples can have a healthy divorce, even if they didn't have a healthy marriage. Joint counseling can be invaluable in helping them deal with the reality that they will be divorced forever.

My suggestion is twofold. First. If you are contemplating divorce, and children are involved, remember *divorce will not end your relationship*. Nor will it end the conflicts -- it only changes them. Second. If you are already divorced, and children are involved, for the sake of all concerned, resolve to have a healthy divorced relationship.

A good divorce is not an oxymoron. It can and does happen. With strong desire and intense determination, a good divorce can be a reality. The end result for everyone is well worth the effort.

Chapter 7

Hold Off On Buying The Rope

He had decided to commit suicide. Made a plan to hang himself. Went to buy the rope. Looking at the variety of rope materials, he found himself choosing a rope that wouldn't hurt his neck!

Telling me this story in a therapy session, he said, "Realizing I was picking a rope that wouldn't hurt my neck, I had a sudden awareness, *I didn't want to stop living, I just wanted to stop hurting.*"

What an awesome discovery!

The same is true for a high percentage of those who take their own lives. Being in such deep emotional pain, ending life seems like the only way to stop the suffering. They are literally "killing the pain."

Psychological researchers perceive that everyone is a potential suicidal candidate, and those who contend they "...would never do such a thing" are in denial. I'm not so sure that it's a universal absolute. However, I do believe the vast majority of adults have or will experience such emotional trauma that the idea of suicide is at least a fleeting thought.

Acknowledging that fact is nothing to be alarmed about. To the contrary, it's rather comforting to know that flashing thoughts and fantasies of taking your own life are not unlike what nearly everyone else has experienced.

One of the compounding problems with having suicidal thoughts is the fear of telling it. Not knowing who to tell, how they will react, or how you will feel after sharing it, prevents disclosure. As a result, those buried feelings don't go away. In fact, they may fester, grow, and escalate into something that's more than a flashing thought. Now, it seems like a real possibility. The thought now includes a plan and a time, and things can really get out of hand from there.

Suicide is a permanent solution to a temporary problem. The key to avoiding such a tragic end is to get some help.

The suicide problem is a multi-faceted catastrophe. In its path is a trail of victims-- spouse, parents, children, siblings, friends, ministers, counselors and the one who suicided.

Over the years, both professionally and personally, I've helped deal with the grief of those left behind. I've felt their pain, and I've experienced my own pain from suicide. The extensive residue nearly always includes an extra measure of guilt, shame, anger, and deep sadness. It's one of the most difficult forms of grief in the human experience.

For emphasis, I repeat. The tragedy of tragedies is that most of the time, *suicide is a permanent solution to a temporary problem.*

Therefore, if you're having such thoughts, have a stroke of sanity. Hold off on buying the rope. Call a suicide hotline, talk to a counselor, parent, spouse, minister, or tell a friend.

Take the yellow pages and start calling counselors until you reach one who can see you immediately. Go to a hospital emergency room. Tell the truth. Don't cover it up or just drop a clue. Tell it all. Get some help.

You don't have to stop living in order to stop hurting.

Chapter 8

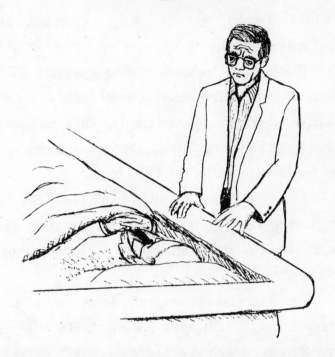

Some Things You Miss, You Miss Forever

As a nationally known surgeon, Daniel had been elected to prestigious positions by his colleagues. For many years, he taught at a distinguished medical school. As an innovator, he had done pioneer work in cardiovascular surgery, and taught his techniques to medical students. He was highly intelligent, very personable, and quite successful. Now, at age fifty-nine, Daniel was seriously depressed, and marginally suicidal.

Under the guise of "going away for CEU" (continuing education units), Daniel spent a week in intensive therapy. (How tragic, that so many professionals including doctors, lawyers, and ministers must get therapy under the CEU banner!)

To say the least, Daniel wasn't really keen on doing therapy. As he put it, "I've always managed my own affairs. I'm smart enough to work out my own problems."

He had taken several doses of a mild antidepressant, but it hadn't worked. His wife was "preposterous enough to propose therapy!" Actually, she had given him an ultimatum, "Get therapy or get out." That was after she had said, "I'm sick of being with someone who is chronically depressed, living in denial, and making my life miserable."

Prior to trying the medication, Daniel had tried other women. His wife suspected it. She confronted him. He confessed. After his two brief affairs, he was still depressed.

Daniel's wife had forgiven him for the infidelities, and still wanted to hold the marriage together. But living with someone who was chronically depressed had pushed her to the limit. After the medication had not worked, she delivered the power punch, "Get therapy or get out!" (Desperation is not the ideal motivator, but sometimes the only one that works.)

Throughout the first three hours of Daniel's intensive, he was defensive and argumentative. He deflected my questions about the hurts, hates, and horrors of his life. He wanted to talk about "his nagging wife, the pressures of modern medicine, the state of world affairs."

We were going nowhere fast. Searching for a clue, I told him the story of an airline pilot who said to his passengers, "I have good news and bad news. The bad news is, all our navigational equipment is out. We have no idea where we are. We are totally lost. The good news is, we're making good time!"

With a heavy trace of sarcasm, he retorted, "You're the pilot. It's up to you to get on the right course!"

Keeping a grip on my own irritation, I took a shot in the dark.

Earlier in the session, Daniel had told me his father had been dead for five years, but he ignored my follow-up questions. So, I said, "Daniel, *some things you miss, you miss forever*. I doubt you ever had your father's approval. But unless you're willing to stop playing mental ping pong and tell me about it, I can't get us on the right course. It's time for lunch. You take a break and think about it. I'll see you in an hour."

At exactly 1:00 p.m., he walked into my therapy room. His eyes were red and swollen. He looked pale and his hair was wet from sweat. He was still standing as he shook his finger at me. Then he spoke.

With a trembling voice, he said, "Don Doyle, you're a son-of-a-bitch. I didn't come here to talk about my father. I came to talk about my wife. I can't remember the last time I cried. But I've been crying ever since I walked out of here an hour ago. I can't stop."

He paused, sat down, blew his nose, and stared at the floor. I remained silent. After a while, he looked up and with a faint smile, said, "So, I gotta talk about it, right? I hope we're on the right course!"

I said, "We are, and now we're really making good time!" Both of us laughed.

For the next few hours (and a couple of days after), Daniel opened up the broken heart of a little boy with a deep "father wound."

His father had been highly successful in the automobile business. At one time, he was the largest Ford dealer in the Northwest. He wanted his son to follow in his footsteps.

Daniel's interest in medicine brought steady harassment from his father. "You can't make any BIG money practicing medicine. You'll work yourself to death for nothing."

Even after Daniel had practiced medicine for many years, the old man frequently said, "When are you gonna get a real job and make some BIG money?"

Why was the old man so opposed to medicine? Because his own father had been a doctor. And an alcoholic. Who abandoned his family. He had squandered his life away in a rural area of Oregon making $5.00 house calls. Daniel's father hated his own doctor-father, and all doctors for that matter. Frequently, he would say, "I've never been in a hospital, nor seen a doctor." And he never forgave Daniel for becoming one.

During one of Daniel's sessions, I asked him to close his eyes, and tell me what he remembered about his father's death (which you recall had occurred five years prior.)

As if it had just been retrieved on a computer screen, he began telling me every detail. The most powerful part occurred the night before the funeral.

After all the visitors had departed, Daniel went

back into the viewing room and closed all the doors.

Looking into the casket at his father, Daniel said the words came out spontaneously and audibly, "You old bastard. You're lying there looking very peaceful. I'm left here knowing that I never did please you. And now, I'll never, *ever* be able to get your approval. And I hate you for that!"

From the day his father died, Daniel was on the road to depression. Of course, with such a gaping *father wound*, he had been on that road all his life. However, his father's death was the catalyst that brought it all to the surface.

Some things you miss, you miss forever. That doesn't mean it's hopeless. However, it does mean perhaps it's time to-- *face the truth and rub your nose in it.*

Feeling is for healing. Purging yourself of the hurts, hates, and horrors of your past can free you to live in the here and now. You can heal. You can make healthy adjustments.

Daniel did. Finally.

Chapter 9

Unsensible Blame

In his book <u>The Streets of Laredo</u> (the sequel to his classic <u>Lonesome Dove</u>), Larry McMurtry has the character "Pea Eye" say, "People aren't sensible in assigning or assuming blame."

What a succinct statement to express a powerful truth. People aren't sensible in assigning or assuming blame. (I wish I'd said that!)

Many relationships that involve addictions are classic illustrations of this truth. The user frequently *assigns the blame* for the addiction to the spouse. Quite often, the spouse cooperates with that assessment by *assuming the blame.*

Wife-beaters explain their actions with only a mild disclaimer. "It was just a little misunderstanding. I shouldn't have hit her, but *she made me do it."*

She in turn will say, "It's my fault. I shouldn't have said what I did. *I know how he is."*

He assigns her the blame, and she assumes it. Such a blame cycle may continue for years.

In the biblical story of the Garden of Eden, Adam assigns blame to Eve. "The woman made me do it." She assigns blame to the serpent. "The serpent made me do it." And pardon the pun-- the snake didn't have a leg to stand on.

A recovering alcoholic clergyman, with whom I worked, was dealing with his neurotic habit of blaming everyone but himself for his actions. He remembered a very interesting story.

The experience had occurred several years earlier. One week after being released from a thirty-day addiction treatment program, Bob attended Sunday morning worship at a church of a different faith.

By circumstance or providence, he picked a church that used wine during communion, rather than the Welch's grape juice from his own tradition.

Kneeling at the altar, he sipped a tablespoon of wine from the Holy chalice. He remembered a rush of emotion that came over him when he thought, "Great! At last I can blame God. All it takes is this little bit of alcohol, and I'm back on the drunk road. And God will be to blame for me using this time."

As he walked back to his seat with a slight sneer on his face, he said he heard a voice. Not an audible voice but a loud inner voice, "Bob, don't you think it's time you stopped the blame game?! You can use it again if you choose. But no one is to blame but *you*!"

That was the final hurdle in his recovery. Fifteen years later, he was still sober.

Why is blame assigned or assumed in such an unsensible manner? Because it was taught in just the same unsensible manner. The tap root of irrational blaming (self or others) is usually found in the house of the family of origin. The place where guilt, fear, anger, and shame were plentiful. Ironically, those prone to be assigners of blame, or assumers of blame, grew up in the same type environment.

Swimming through childhood in a sea of guilt, fear, anger, or shame you either emerge *assigning* or *assuming* blame.

And you will take your cue from whichever parent unconsciously impacted you the most. Not necessarily the parent you liked the best, but the one that more forcefully impacted your personality.

When it comes to assuming or assigning blame, people just aren't sensible. Processing that truth could be the first hurdle toward resolving your problem.

Whatever the dilemma-- breaking the blame game is a step in the right direction.

One of my favorite maxims applies to both the **ASSUMERS** and **ASSIGNERS** of blame.

You are not responsible for being the way you are, but you are totally responsible for doing something about it.

Chapter 10

The Marriage Wheel

During frontier days, roadways often had signs that read something like the following:

PICK YOUR RUTS WELL,
YOU'LL BE IN THEM FOR THE NEXT
100 MILES!

Many people who get into relational therapy can certainly identify with this perplexity. They express such complaints as: "We're stuck." "We're in a rut." "Nothing ever changes." "We never move forward." "We've started over, again and again, only to end up back in the same old rut."

A few years ago, I conducted a therapy session with a couple who offered many of the above complaints.

While listening to them, it occurred to me that the wheel is a good metaphor for marriage. Later, I developed *The Marriage Wheel* as a method for evaluating a relationship.

Every marriage or intimate relationship connects in five different areas, which become the five spokes in the wheel.

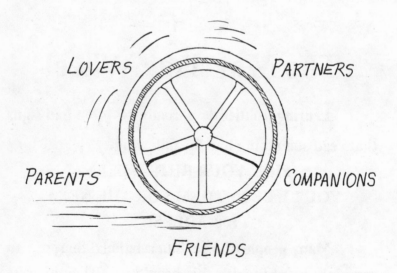

PARTNERS is the spoke in the wheel that shares responsibilities, such as finances, chores, and the mundane tasks of living. She pays the bills; he makes dinner. He takes care of yard work; she does the laundry. She plans vacations; he runs the vacuum. These may be done jointly. Tradeouts may be negotiated. But every couple develops some sort of partnership for taking care of business.

***

COMPANIONS is the spoke in the wheel that shares activities. Companion comes from the Latin root words-- *cum* (together) and *panis* (bread). Literally speaking, a *companion is one with whom you break bread or share a meal.* Interestingly enough, we seldom initiate having a meal with someone we don't like.   The companion spoke means enjoying hanging out together, spending time together. Going to movies and concerts, watching television, playing backgammon, exercising, backpacking, fishing together.

In the early stages of a relationship, it is common to hear: "The reason I like her is because we have so much in common." Most of the time, this means they enjoy the same activities-- they're good companions.

***

FRIENDS is the spoke in the wheel that shares feelings. Friends share hopes, dreams, wants, needs, and desires. Friends share fear, affection, anger, and hurt. When friends share a sorrow, the sadness is halved. When friends share joy, the celebration is doubled.

The Arabian proverb says it well: "A friend is one to whom you pour out your heart, wheat and chaff together. Knowing that with the gentlest of hands, that which is worth keeping will be saved and that which needs to be discarded will be blown away."

Friends are for feelings.

***

LOVERS is the spoke in the wheel that shares the physical, the sexual, the erotic, the romantic, the passionate. It includes light body rubs and deep massages. It means snuggling, cuddling, touching, being naked and not ashamed.

Lovers touch. Many people are *skin starved* from lack of touching. Lovers feed the skin, the largest organ in the human body.

Lovers are in the business of pleasuring each other in every way that is acceptable to both. Using all the senses-- sight, sound, smell, taste, touch-- lovers pleasure each other.

***

PARENTS is the spoke in the wheel that shares childcare. This could also include nurturing each other, in healthy ways. But primarily, it means sharing the responsibilities of parenting your offspring. The span of parenting goes from conception to commencement, and includes all the obvious things that go with this task.

***

A marriage with five strong spokes will be unusually harmonious. To be sure, such a relationship is not stuck and not in a rut. That couple is definitely moving forward.

With four spokes working effectively, there's probably only minimal complaint. With three, there will be some conflict. However, a wheel with three spokes still may be able to move forward at a slow pace. When only one or two spokes are working without conflict, that relationship is in a deep rut. When there are *no* strong spokes, the tire is flat. And you can be sure that relationship is stuck, and there is no movement.

One of the most amazing things often comes out of therapy. Relationships that are stuck in a rut have the potential to get into a *groove.*

A rut and a groove may look the same, but obviously they're not. It will take some hard work that is usually quite painful. But it may not be as far from a rut to a groove as you think.

Using the marriage wheel metaphor, how would you rate your relationship?

Chapter 11

"Don't I Know You?"

That's what she said, when I walked up hurriedly to the hotel checkout desk. Actually, it wasn't a question; it was more of a statement.

"Don't I know you? Well, of course I do. I just saw you on television," she said, pointing to a small screen in the corner. Good sermon, mister. I liked what you said about God working through people. I've always believed that myself."

"Thank you very much," I said, "Your words

are very kind. I've enjoyed being here. I hope to come back sometime."

Anxiously, I tossed a credit card on the counter. I heard two strikes from the grandfather clock. My flight was scheduled to leave in less than an hour. I didn't have much time to spare. With any delays, it was going to be close.

She picked up the VISA card and began the checkout procedure. Then she said, "My father was a minister, but he never preached on television!"

Now, freeze the frame. Hold that image for a moment while I put this conversational transaction in context.

The three-day seminar I had just led was entitled "Peer Counselor Training Conference." For the first two days, I had worked fervently with fifty people who wanted to develop their skills in doing informal spontaneous counseling. They had listened intently, taken copious notes, (well, some of them, at least) and had practiced with each other. I had given several demos on "How To Do It." They were quick studies. Enjoyable to work with. I was feeling good.

The workshop had ended with all fifty participants pledging to "listen for the heart cries of the hurting masses." And whenever opportunities arose, they would minister to those needs in the peer counseling fashion.

The final sessions were on Sunday. Along with a television audience, approximately six hundred people had shared in the worship experience. They had responded quite favorably to my presentations concerning "the way God works through the hands of people."

As peer counselors, they had determined to make an impact in their community, an elegant old city in the Southwest.

Now, reroll the film and you will have the previous part of this story in the proper perspective.

The lady at the checkout counter had said, "My father was a minister."

To insure that I wouldn't miss my flight, I was tempted to ignore the *glaring KEY word* in this peer counseling opportunity. But I had spent three days talking about developing sensitivity to peer counseling opportunities. I had taught them to hear those KEY words. I succumbed to my own teaching.

"Did you say WAS?" I asked. Thus, began fifteen minutes of conversational catharsis.

"Yes, he's been dead for twenty years," she said. She looked back at the computer screen.

"That's a long time," I responded. "You must have been quite young."

"I was only fifteen," she said. Her chin quivered, voice cracked, and eyes watered.

"What happened to him?" I continued.

"Killed in a train wreck." Tears were flowing down her cheeks.

"Still hurts, doesn't it?" I said.

"Like hell!" she blurted out. "Guess I'd forgotten how much. Don't know what's wrong with me. Sorry, about swearing."

"No need to apologize. Sometimes it takes strong language to express strong feelings. Old wounds are hard to heal, and yours still hurts, doesn't it?"

"Darn right," she said. The tears came again.

"I know you loved your father, and after all these years still miss him."

"Yes, I loved him very much and really do miss him. He was a good daddy!"

My checkout was now completed. "What caused the accident?" I asked.

Quite composed, she said, "His car stalled on the tracks, just south of town. He was only forty. I haven't cried over him in years. Thanks for listening. Hope I didn't detain you."

"Not at all," I said stepping around the counter. As I gave her a hug I said, "You take care of yourself, and tell someone else about how much you miss your daddy."

It had taken nearly twenty minutes to check out. As I got into the car, my host and driver said, "Man we're really late. What in the world took you so long?"

Looking back at the hotel, I said, "Oh, just a twenty-year-old train wreck."

Chapter 12

Just Relax

Over a career that has spanned nearly thirty years, I've spoken thousands of times before groups. None of those experiences is more memorable than a speaking engagement in 1988. That was the year I addressed my father's AA (alcoholics anonymous) group when he received his one-year sobriety chip.

After a person has completed a year of sobriety, a "birthday party" is planned for an *Open Meeting Night*. In some AA groups, it is customary for the honoree to invite a speaker for the evening. My father chose me.

I've never been prouder of my father than the night he got his one-year chip. I've never been more honored than having been asked to speak. Only a few times during speaking engagements have I ever been as nervous!

Days before the event, as I was trying to prepare, I was feeling extreme anxiety. I was worried about what I would say, and how I would say it.

My plan was to find a theme that would be relevant to the occasion. My brother, Mickey, suggested that I use the subject "Dead Hogs and No Hot Water." My tentative topic was "Getting More Living Out of Life." I thought his idea sounded better. However, I couldn't work up the courage to try it.

The anxiety I was feeling was grossly interfering with the preparation. I kept telling myself to *take a deep breath and just relax*. I was employing the same techniques I'd used countless times to help control my *performance anxiety*. Nothing worked.

Finally, I had a stroke of sanity. I knew what I would say to the *Open AA Group* meeting-- "RELAX, JUST RELAX." I'd make the word *relax* into an acronym. It worked. I've been using it in therapy for stress management ever since. Here's what I said.

R-- RELEASE your emotional trash every day. Before going to bed each night, take inventory of the day. Release all the heartache, worry, frustration, disappointment, and resentment. Give them up to God, your Higher Power, the Spirit that's bigger than life-- whatever feels right to you. But do not take into tomorrow the residue from today.

E-- ENJOY the moment. It's all you've got. *Regrets about the past and fear of the future destroy the present.* Celebrate every gorgeous moment. Don't let yesterday or tomorrow distract from today. Live in the here and now.

L-- LAUGH long and loud every day. It's good medicine for the body, mind, and soul.

Laughter is the shortest distance between two people. Start by laughing at yourself, which will help others to laugh at themselves. Laugh every day.

If you find it difficult or awkward to laugh, you may need to *prime your laughing pump*. Listen to tapes, watch videos, and read books that make you laugh. Keep these tools of laughter close at hand and use them.

(When I speak before groups, I always use some form of humor, and I'm always looking for those who can't laugh. They concern me because losing your sense of humor is a clear sign of big trouble.)

A-- ACCEPT your imperfection and the imperfection in others. Few things bring more stress and strife than perfectionism. Perfectionism is not about doing things well. *Perfectionism is about never being satisfied with how you or someone else performs.*

Perfectionism often destroys spontaneity, hampers creativity, and frequently ruins relationships.

Perfectionism is a major contributor to the development of phobias, addictions, depression, and compulsivity. The good news? *Perfectionism was learned and it can be unlearned.*

X-- X OUT worrying about the small stuff. (You're right, I had to force the acronym a bit, but it still works.) Cross out or X out unnecessary concern about things that don't really matter. The old adage says it quite well:

LESSON ONE. Don't Sweat the Small Stuff.
LESSON TWO.   It's All Small Stuff.

Actually, it's not all small stuff. A catastrophe is not small stuff. But most of us spend a lot of energy catastrophizing about things that are not catastrophes. All too often, we mountain climb over mole hills.

Roger was a client who needed to relax. He told me about his father who was always tense and stressed about even the most insignificant issues. Roger wondered if he might have taken his father's lead in getting so stressed out over trivial matters.

"Roger," I said, "It sounds like your dad was really uptight about everything."

"Uptight!?" he responded, "He was so uptight, you couldn't drive a nail in his behind with a ball peen hammer!"

That's uptight! Maybe you're not that bad. But nearly all of us can benefit from learning to stop worrying about the small stuff.

My encouragement to you (and to myself) is to **RELAX:**

Release your trash every day.

Enjoy the moment.

Laugh loud and long.

Accept imperfection.

X out worrying about the small stuff.

✱✱✱

If you've got *Dead Hogs and No Hot Water*, mastering these five tasks may not solve your dilemma. But learning to **RELAX** will certainly reduce the stress from such a predicament. Undoubtedly, consistent relaxation could help all of us *Get More Living Out of Life.*

Maybe St. Paul was saying he had learned to RELAX, when he wrote:

"I have learned whatsoever state I am in, thereby to be content."

***

I'm not sure what I had to say at the AA meeting was helpful to those in attendance. But it surely helped me.

Chapter 13

Can You Trust Feelings?

Although he was quite articulate and intelligent, the young man from Arkansas had a history of doing some really dumb things. The latest episode included leaving his wife and two kids for another woman. His explanation? "I'm not in love with my wife anymore. I'm in love with this other woman. I'm outta here. I'm going with my feelings."

My question to him. "Can you trust your feelings?"

He looked puzzled but didn't answer. "What makes you think you can trust your feelings?" I repeated. "Maybe they're lying to you?!"

Feelings frequently lie to us. They tell us things are dangerous, when they aren't. Make us feel guilt, when we're not guilty. Prompt us to feel rage, over things that aren't outrageous. Feelings often lie to us.

Current feelings are often contaminated with *primal pain from childhood and accumulated conflicts from adulthood.* Unless you have cleaned out your childhood hurts and discharged your adult conflicts, you can count on it-- your feelings will deceive you.

Take romantic feelings. "How do you know this is the right person for you?"

"Well, down deep I just have this feeling that it's right." Careful. That deep inner feeling might be gas!

Several years ago, Kenny Rogers had a hit song with a chorus that said, "I'm on fire with morning desire." Early one morning, I felt a little romantic. I snuggled up close to my wife and whispered, "I'm on fire with morning desire."

She responded, "Take a couple of Rolaids and go back to sleep!"

Few things are dumber than acting on feelings which are still tainted with unresolved hurts, hates, and horrors from the past.

In addition, many of us have been so conditioned to hide our feelings that we lie to ourselves and others about what we feel.

For example, take anger. Numerous people were shamed in childhood about anger. As adults they don't even know they feel it. That's *repression*. The feeling has been denied for so long, you don't even have access to it.

Sometimes I'll ask a person, who is oozing with anger, "Are you angry?" "No. "Resentful?" "No." "Aggravated?" "No." "Irritated?" "Well, maybe a little." "Whew!"

On the other hand, *suppression* is knowing you have the feeling and choosing not to express it. There may be any number of good reasons to keep your feelings to yourself. The circumstances may dictate the wisdom of sharing or suppressing. When this is the case, a little assertiveness training can be very helpful. But when you have repressed your feelings, you don't even know you have them.

Many of our senior citizen mothers qualify for the *Repressed Anger Club*-- my own included.

My mother very successfully owned and

operated <u>Zula's</u>, a women's clothing store, for nearly twenty-five years.

One day, a customer took the liberty of advising my mother about the store. "You've got too much merchandise," she volunteered. "It's not properly displayed."

Although this woman had never owned or managed a business in her life, the self-appointed, clothing-store-consultant continued, "You'd be more successful if you ran the store better."

In a condescending and sarcastic tone, she went on, "What you ought to do is change the store's image."

The entire exchange was uncalled for, extremely inappropriate, and rude. Socially unacceptable behavior.

When my mother related this story to me over the phone, it had been a couple of days since the incident occurred. I was livid. "That really ticks me off," I blurted out. "I can't believe she said that to you! Who does she think she is?! Didn't that make you angry?"

My mother responded, "I think it did."

"Did you tell her?" I asked.

"No," she replied.

"Why not? Why did you choose not to let her

know that it made you angry?"

Mother responded, "I didn't know it till now!"

God love her. She's just the greatest mother in the whole world. But like so many women from her generation, she has repressed anger forever. Often doesn't even know she is feeling it.

If senior citizen women ever allow themselves to express anger-- look out!

On the other hand, not everyone has that problem. Sometimes it's interesting to meet a person who knows how they feel and owns it. Vernon was one such person.

For two years, while I was a seminary student, I was privileged to be the pastor of Beech Fork Church at Gravel Switch, Kentucky.

Within the first month in that position, I was recruited by family members to retrieve their dear brother, Vernon, from his backsliding ways.

They said God Almighty had chosen me "...to be the one to turn our precious brother's life around."

Wow! How could I have been so lucky to get such an assignment? I was quite naive. Much later, I realized that for twenty years they had told every new minister the same story! Nonetheless, they threw the bait, and I bit.

One Sunday afternoon, bright-eyed and bushy-tailed, I went out to *save* brother Vernon. He was a farmer. I found him out in the pasture repairing some fencing. After a few moments of small talk, I got right to the point. "Vernon, why don't you come to church?"

With noticeable annoyance he said, "Cause I don't want to!"

I stood there speechless at his response. I had never heard such an honest answer. Yes, at that time, I was new in the business. However, in a dozen years following, I never heard that answer again.

He went on. "You know, I could give you a bunch of excuses, but I'd be walking around you, just like you did them cow patties getting out here."

With a louder voice and with a sharper edge, he went on, "But the truth is, I don't go to church 'cause I don't want to. If I wanted to, I'd go. And if I ever want to, I will. But I don't want to. So I don't."

It didn't take me long to find my way back to the car. So much for being God's chosen one to save brother Vernon!

At least it was interesting and somewhat refreshing, to meet someone who knew how he felt, owned it, and expressed it.

However, I would later discover that Vernon, like many others, could only express one feeling-- *anger.*

When it comes to feelings, some people only have access to one. What is your emotion of choice? That is, during a conflict or crisis, what emotion do you experience most frequently? Fear? Guilt? Sadness? Anger? Never thought about it? Well, think about it. During a negative experience, what are you likely to feel?

Traditionally and tragically, our culture has *trained women to be hurt and men to be angry.* How absurd and unhealthy. The reason it's so ridiculous is because-- *you can never be hurt enough to get rid of anger, nor angry enough to get rid of hurt.*

Trying to discharge all feelings through one emotion is like trying to empty a bathtub with an eye dropper. It's not going to work.

Feelings *can not* be trusted. They lied to the Arkansas traveler who left his wife and children for another woman. Feelings will lie to you, as well.

Feelings are to be felt, owned, shared, and processed. But you'd better be careful about acting on your feelings. Such action has produced loads of suffering for countless people.

Chapter 14

Easy On The Eyes

In an old Larry Gatlin song, the chorus said: "On top of all the good she is, Lord, she's mighty easy on the eyes."

Being attracted to the physical appearance of a mate is an important ingredient in a marriage relationship. But being *easy on the eyes* isn't nearly as likely to produce a healthy relationship as *being easy to live with*.

At age sixteen, I read my first book about

marriage. It was given to me by George Capps, my minister and friend. Written by David Mace, the book was entitled, <u>Whom God Hath Joined</u>.

From then until now, in and out of the therapy room, I've observed countless relationships. Perhaps more important, I've been married to the same woman since 1963. My conclusion is that *being easy to live with* is the glue that holds marriages together, provides fulfillment and contentment, and allows for growth.

To be sure, many relationships stay together when one or the other isn't easy to be with. Sometimes, they may be down right hard to live with. However, these relationships seldom grow, quite often are volatile, and usually don't produce very much fulfillment.

Some marriage partners are *high maintenance* people. They want much, need much, expect much, require much. Others are *low maintenance* people. They don't want much, need much, expect much, or require much.

High maintenance people are usually dependent on others for their emotional well-being. *Low maintenance* people generally cooperate with that dependency.

To assume high or low maintenance people are right or wrong, good or bad, would be a misconception. The high maintenance and low maintenance phraseology is just a means of evaluating why some relationships work better than others. Observing relationships through these lenses, may be very insightful and therapeutic.

However, it is true that high maintenance people are not as easy to be with as low maintenance people. They are inclined to criticize, want to control, and try to change their mates. Low maintenance people are open to criticism, may not mind being controlled, and often make changes to please the spouse.

A few years ago, I watched a television interview with a well-known, high profile couple. I said to my wife, "That's a bigtime, high maintenance relationship! Both of them want much, need much, expect much, and require much. I'll bet they won't be married five years." They split up in three.

High maintenance people aren't generally easy to be with. When two are in the same marriage, it can be hell on wheels. Such a combination isn't hopeless. However, if two people who are both high maintenance develop a good relationship, it will require an extra measure of determination and commitment.

One of our family's wisest and most remarkable people is my wife's uncle by marriage, John Houston.

One of his endearing traits is how he shows affection. The men and boys he calls "Bo." The girls and women he calls "Sister." (All of us love it.)

When John was in his mid-seventies, I took him to see my new office suite. We sat down and talked for a while about the work I do in relational therapy. He asked several extremely good questions about couples who come in for therapy.

After a while, he said, "Bo, over the years I've noticed that marriages have *givers* and *takers*. When two givers get together, they have a great thing going. When a giver and a taker are together, they can do pretty well, too. But when two takers get together, look out!"

Regarding relationships, I've read many books, heard numerous lectures, and delivered my fair share of them. And that's about as accurate and wise as it gets. *Easy on the eyes isn't nearly as important as being easy to live with.* Thanks, John.

Chapter 15

"Whachuruninfrum?"

What is a mid-life crisis? How do you know if you're having one? Can you have more than one? Is it just a man thing?

For starters, the mid-life crisis is more stage than age, occurring anywhere from late twenty's to late fifty's. Two men with whom I've worked, illustrate my point.

Both men were high achievers, and had risen to the top of their professions. Each had run their own companies. Both had lived exemplary lives. When they came for intensive therapy, both were engaged in some bizarre out-of-character behavior. One was twenty-nine, the other fifty-nine.

Neither of these men was literally in the middle years. The first had not reached the middle. The second had long since passed it. Both had the earmarks of the *middle age crazies*. The mid-life crisis *really is* more stage than age.

No, it's not just a man thing. Women are equal candidates for the middlesence turning point. Especially in today's world. In the past ten years, I've seen many women who were dealing with the struggles of the middle years.

And yes, you can have more than one. I've had several, myself. The first one started when I had my thirtieth birthday, and I became quite conscious of my *physical appearance, and the lack of adventure in my life.*

One day while wearing nothing but a pair of boxers, I looked in the mirror and couldn't find my chest. "What happened to my chest!?" I blurted out to no one. "I once had a pretty impressive physique! What happened to my chest?"

Grabbing the tape measure soon revealed the awesome truth. My chest was in my shorts!

My measurements had once been 44-33-38. Now, they were more like 33-38-44. Horror of horrors, my chest had dropped into my shorts. It had fallen from grace!

At that exact moment, I had a flashback of being in the locker-room of a health club. Two older men were standing buck-naked waiting to get on the scales. One said, "Arnie, you're old, fat, and ugly!"

Arnie replied, "Ralph, I may be old and fat, but I'm not ugly."

Ralph persisted, "Well, you can believe me, ugly's coming!"

As I looked around in my shorts to find my chest, it struck me that Ralph was a very wise man.

Growing up, I had always wanted to be six feet two inches tall, and weigh two hundred pounds. However, at one hundred and fifty-five pounds, and five feet nine inches tall, in the eleventh grade, I stopped growing taller. Now at age thirty, I had reached half my childhood dream! I was tipping the scales two hundred and ten pounds. Desperately, I tried to convince myself that one out of two wasn't so bad. It didn't work. So, I went on a diet. Started working out. Bought a pair of *Nike* waffle trainers, and began running. Actually, I was jogging. There IS a big difference.

One day while jogging, I passed a couple of nine-year-old boys in the neighborhood who knew me as "Mr. Don." They were shooting marbles.

One jumped up and started jogging along beside me. While sweat was pouring, and I was gasping for breath, he said: "Mr. Don, what are you running from?" The way he said it was all one word, *"Whachuruninfrum?"*

"Old age, Wilson," I whispered.

"Shoot," he said laughing, and turned back to his partner to continue playing marbles. (Actually, "shoot" is not what he said, but it's pretty close.)

Thirty minutes later, I had made the loop. The boys were still shooting marbles. I was a lot closer to death.

When Wilson saw me, he laid his head back and laughed really loud and said, "Whachuruninfrum this time, Mr. Don?!"

Muttering under my breath, I said, "Shut up Wilson!"

During my first mid-life crisis, I lost some weight. With a lot of work, I got in pretty good shape, and retrieved at least part of my chest. However, I was still bothered by the *lack of adventure in my life issue.* So, I did what numerous male mid-lifers do-- bought a motorcycle.

There are two types of mid-life men who buy motorcycles. Those who always wanted one, whose mother wouldn't allow it. And those who had one as a teenager, and need to relive it. Having ridden a motorcycle during my youth, I was in the latter grouping. During my first mid-life crisis, I needed to re-experience my teens, so I bought a Honda 550.

Men who ride motorcycles love to rub other men's noses in it. When they approach traffic lights, they look for old station wagons and mini vans. They enjoy pulling up beside a man in a vehicle full of crying kids and a wife who is giving him hell.

The *van guy* will look at the *bike guy* and shake his head, just a little. The *bike guy* will look at the *van guy* and smile, just a little. Then the *bike guy* will invariably "rev" up the engine a couple of times.

Without speaking a word, here is what they have communicated. The *van guy* has said, "I wish I were you!" And the *bike guy* has said, "Hang in there, buddy!"

Men have a strange attraction to motorcycles. Maybe a motorcycle is a primordial, surrogate horse. The majority of our forefathers rode horses. We straddle motorcycles. Strangely enough, I'm afraid of horses. Only ridden five times in my life. Got thrown on three of those outings! That's enough to make you afraid. But I'm not afraid of *motorhorses,* and have always been attracted to them.

My brother, Mickey, has a theory that *all men want to BUY a motorcycle.* He has one that he doesn't ride. He's ridden only a hundred and fifty miles in four years. He won't sell it though, because he says, "Having a motorcycle, even if I don't ride it, keeps me from wanting to *buy* one!" Now, that's smart.

Well, I rode the Honda 550 for two years and a few thousand miles. I felt better-- I guess.

Recently, a friend asked me if the mid-life crisis was real, or just an excuse people use for doing stupid things?

Some of both, I suspect.

Chapter 16

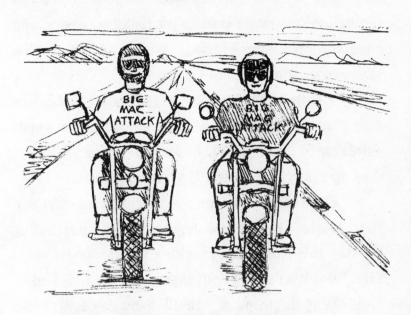

The Big Mac Attack

My second mid-life crisis occurred in my late-thirties and resulted in moving to California to work. My third male-menopause prompted me to move back to the South in my mid-forties. But moving back to Dixie, didn't solve the recurring need for more adventure in my life issue. So, I bought another motorcycle.

Unlike the first motorcycle venture, this was big time. Bought a *Goldwing* 1100. (That's big!)

Along with Jerry Wagley, my old college

roommate and fraternity brother, we rode 3500 miles through the mountain states. We took two weeks, and rode through New Mexico, Arizona, Utah, Idaho, Wyoming, Montana, and Colorado.

I called the trip *The Big MAC (Middle Age Crazy) Attack.* Had T-shirts made up with those words emblazoned on the front. Believe me when I tell you, the trip really had some **CRAZY** moments.

Our first day out, we went through Las Cruces, New Mexico. It was 106 degrees at 6:00 p.m. After hearing this story, a man with a meteorologist voice said, "But it's dry heat out there. It's not that bad."

Why do people say that? Why do people from Arizona and New Mexico always say that? Especially Phoenix. All people from Phoenix say, "Yes, our weather is hot, but it's dry heat."

Let me tell you something. When we moved to California in 1979, we went through the Mojave desert. It was 118 degrees of dry heat, and it was hot, hot, hot. It was so hot we couldn't use the air conditioner because *Old Bertha* (our station wagon) would overheat.

With the windows down, we were stifled by the dry heat. So we, like the vacationing Griswalds, drove West from Needles, California, in 118 degrees with the windows up. Devoted wife and super mom,

Martha, dipped towels in the cooler to rub on our faces and necks to deal with that dry heat!

Let me give you another tip at no charge. Riding a motorcycle in 106 degree weather is hot! In fact, it will suck the water out of your skin till you look like a California raisin.

Back to the *Big Mac Attack*. Four days after being in the sweltering dry heat of New Mexico, we were were in Montpelier, Idaho. It was 25 degrees at 8:00 a.m.

The man with the meteorologist voice heard this part of the story, also. He followed his brilliant platitude, "but it's dry heat" with a question. "How do you stay warm in 25 degree weather on a motorcycle?"

I said, "Oh, it was a dry cold! It wasn't that bad." (The truth? We froze! Nearly to death!)

We went through several rain storms, and one hail storm, which I only need to do once. Rode through Yellowstone Park in several inches of new fallen snow. It was a great trip with loads of interesting experiences. One occurred in southern Utah.

We had ridden the east rim of the Grand Canyon and headed north. It was late in the afternoon. We were looking for a place to spend the night. All the motels either had no vacancies, or looked like places we didn't want to stay. So, we decided to ride to Page, Arizona. We fantasized about getting a nice room, soaking in a jacuzzi, and relaxing.

The desert night air was really cold. By the time we got to Page, it was 9:00 p.m. We were frozen. Guess what? There was no room in the Holiday Inn, the Ramada Inn, nor at any other place in Page. A convention had tied up every room in the whole city.

At this point, you can be sure that we were not happy mid-lifers seeking *more adventure in our lives.* In fact, it was at that very moment that I had a flashback of what a man had said to me about riding a motorcycle.

I had been visiting my brother, Chris. (He's the baby of our family, and one of my favorite people in the whole world.) When I came out to leave, his neighbor was looking at my motorcycle.

"Ain't that thing dangerous?" asked the neighbor.

"Yes, it is," I said.

"Ain't it hot in the summer?" he continued.

"Yes, it is," I repeated.

"Probably cold in the winter, too?" he surmised.

"You're still right," I nodded.

"Bet you get nasty, riding it?" he persisted.

"You're batting a thousand," I said.

Shaking his head, he concluded, "Don't believe I'd want one of 'em!"

"No, I'm sure you wouldn't!!" I confirmed. Then I proceeded to rub it in, just a little.

"Sir, when you look at this machine, you see, danger, hot, cold, nasty. When I look at it, I see beauty, freedom, individuality." Dramatically, I polished my speech off with distinct smugness. "When I'm riding this machine, and smelling the rush of fresh air, it feels like I'm riding the wind."

My smugness not withstanding, I stand before one and all to offer a *true confession*. On the cold night we left Page, Arizona, because there was *no room in the inn*, I couldn't remember what I had self-righteously told that man. But I vividly remembered his words, "Don't believe I'd want one of 'em!"

A sympathetic hotel clerk at the Ramada Inn, found a vacancy in Big Water, Utah. It was at a fishing lodge. A resort fishing lodge, we surmised.

The call was made and the reservation was secured. We saddled up for the hour-long ride. It was really cold! We were consoled, however, by envisioning a big fireplace, a warm fire, a sauna, a hottub, a cheeseburger, and a longneck Moosehead beer.

Finally, we found the resort fishing lodge. It was not a Four Star Hotel! It was not a hotel, at all. It wasn't even a lodge. There was no fireplace, no fire, no jacuzzi, hottub, cheeseburger, nor longneck Moosehead beer. It was a trailer park with a half dozen mobile homes. OLD and UGLY mobile homes.

According to the hostess, she had only one left, "a two-bedroomer, with hot running water, and carpeted throughout." It was $85.00 per night! Jerry negotiated her down to $80.00, and we unpacked our gear at the Big Water Hilton.

The place was filthy. The carpet had worn out the decade before. It smelled very fishy. All sorts of insects were wandering around. Thank God, the hot water worked.

After checking out the beds for visible varmints, we were ready to call it a night.

Jerry said, "I don't know about you, but I'm sleeping with all my clothes on, including my socks."

"Not me," I responded, "I'm sleeping buck-naked. Whatever gets on your clothes tonight will be with you all day tomorrow. Whatever gets on me tonight, I'll wash off with that hot water in the morning!" (To protect the innocent and the guilty, I will never repeat what he said after that! I will give a hint. It had a lot to do with my family heritage.)

The *Big MAC Attack* was a great experience with many unforgettable moments. There were times when I thought it might have removed forever *the need for more adventure in my life!*

One memorable part of that trip involved a city limit sign in a small town in New Mexico. We saw it at the same time, doubled back, made a picture, and had a good laugh.

The sign read: "Welcome to Portales, New Mexico, Home of 12,493 Friendly Folks and 8 or 10 Old Grouches."

Writing in my journal later that evening, I thought about that strange city limit sign. I concluded, that's probably a pretty accurate assessment of people. Friendly, decent, caring folks greatly outnumber the cantankerous, troublemaking, old grouches.

Sadly, we seldom see or acknowledge this truth. Instead, we spend more of our time-- talking about how bad people are, how terrible the times, and what a mess things are in-- distorting the truth.

Portales, New Mexico, I salute you for telling it like it really is.

Meanwhile, back to the mid-life crisis.

A man in therapy once said to me: "I must be having a mid-life crisis. When I have a day off, I don't know what the hell to do with it."

That's a pretty good start in making a diagnosis. The mid-life crisis is occurring when you start asking,

"Is this all there is?"

"Is this what I've been chasing?"

"Is there no more to life?"

There's an old proverb that says: "If you don't know where you're going, you'll probably end up somewhere else."

That's what the mid-life crisis is really all about. It's about direction, destination, and depression. It's knowing you've lost sight of where you're going, and are afraid you'll end up somewhere else.

The mid-life crisis is not necessarily negative, at all. To be sure, it often includes some *out-of-character* behavior that may be inappropriate. It, also, can certainly be positive.

The essence of the mid-life crisis involves reflection and reassessment of your life. It can be the catalyst for answering three questions:

Who am I?

How did I get that way?

What can I do about it, if I choose?

***

Getting some competent help and using it constructively, the mid-life crisis could be one of the best things that ever happens to you.

Chapter 17

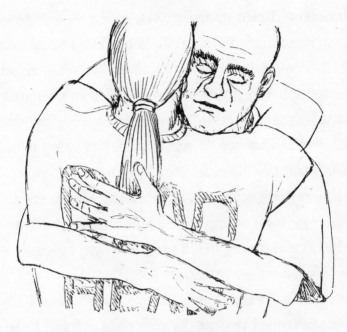

A Chip Off the
Old Block?

The call came to my home rather than the counseling center. It was two days before Christmas.

"Doctor, I'm sorry to bother you at home, especially during the holidays, but I have a crisis and time is of the essence."

Weakly, I assured him it was okay. Knowing that few of the crises calls that came to my home were really crises, I was not very convincing.

Calling from Colorado, he continued, "I have incurable brain cancer. Each of my two businesses generates more than a million a year. I want to turn both companies over to my son. He's twenty-eight years old. The problem is we have been alienated for many years. Can't remember having a decent conversation since he was fifteen. I'm going to die. I don't want to die separated from my son."

I had not given enthusiastic assurance to his apology for calling me at home. After hearing his story, I was feeling like a jerk, and my responses were much more empathic.

He went on, "You have been highly recommended to me by someone whom I deeply respect, and has been to your place for therapy. Doctor, again I apologize for calling you at home during the Christmas holidays; but having heard my story, will you answer three questions? Can you help us? Will you help us? Soon-- very soon?"

My answer was, "Yes, to all of the above. How soon can you be here?"

"We can leave here the day after Christmas. It'll take at least two days in the RV. If we don't kill each other first, we could be there by Monday."

"I'll be waiting," was all I said before hanging up the phone.

Monday morning, bright and early, I met the odd couple from Colorado. What a contrast between a father and a son. To be sure, it was not a case of "my father, my self." Son was definitely not *a chip off the old block.*

Dad wore L.L. Bean gabardine khakis, a monogrammed dress shirt, and brown Lucchesi boots. He wore a Stetson which covered the glaring baldness from chemotherapy. *Son* wore faded Levi 501 jeans, a rattlesnake skin belt, Zodiac boots, and a Grateful Dead tee shirt. Surprisingly, he did wear a Stetson, but it covered a long ponytail that was tucked underneath. And he had an earring.

Dad was a hardworking, conservative, teetotaling Methodist. *Son* was a laid-back dirtbiker, agnostic at best, heavy drinker, and pot smoker.

Dad usually kept the radio on easy listening or gospel, with an occasional touch of Willie or Waylon. *Son* was into the Doobies, (both the group and the joint) the Eagles, and he was a card-carrying Deadhead.

Dad was a decorated World War II veteran, a member of the VFW, American Legion, and always voted Republican. *Son* had supported the Vietnam war resistors; wasn't a member of anything, and had never voted. However, during high school, he was impressed with George McGovern and Eugene McCarthy.

Dad had been driving forty-five years, and never had even a fender bender, or a traffic violation. *Son* had totaled two cars and a truck. In addition, he had acquired enough speeding tickets to fill up a shoe box.

Dad had been married to the same woman for thirty-five years. *Son* had been married and divorced twice. He was working on a third-- marriage and divorce, that is.

For six hours a day, for two weeks in succession, these two men strapped on their emotional seat belts, and laid it all on the table. Unpacking the baggage between them, they got down to the *heart of the matter*. Through some honest, open, hard work, both took giant steps in understanding and forgiveness of each other and themselves.

The reconciliation included an array of feelings of hostility, profanity, and gut-wrenching sobs. An outpouring of affirmations and hugs came later.

One year later, *Dad* died, but he wasn't alienated from his son. *Son* was by his side, carrying on the family tradition.

When it comes to lasting, healthy relationships ,
reconciliation is a regular requirement.

*The heart of the matter is understanding and
forgiveness.*

Chapter 18

Bad Goodbyes

Few things hurt worse than a bad goodbye. Bad goodbyes leave wounds that are slow to heal and scars that are long-term sensitive.

Many adults are excessively fearful of abandonment, panic when alone, and are afraid of the dark. Some are terrified of rejection and tormented with jealousy. Such excessive feelings can usually be traced to a bad goodbye in childhood or early adulthood.

You don't get over bad goodbyes in a short time. Maybe never. Good goodbyes cut deep and clean, like a sharp knife, and healing comes slowly but surely. Bad goodbyes cut like a jagged saw, and the healing is slow and tedious, with flashbacks and setbacks.

Bad goodbyes come from children dying, runaway teens, forced retirement, premature death, being fired, suicide, and most divorces.

At the core of a bad goodbye is an excruciating discovery. I've often heard this awareness expressed in the statement, "I thought I mattered more than that." Oh, that smarts! Cuts to the bone.

Bad goodbyes that occur in adulthood are hard enough to manage. When they happen in childhood, it's much worse. Bad goodbyes that happen to children, leave wounds that get opened up again, and again, through adult experiences.

Let me illustrate with a very personal experience.

When I was three years old, my father was drafted into the army for World War II. My mother took him to the depot. He was to catch the Greyhound for Fort Oglethorpe, Georgia. There was a lot of emotion surrounding that goodbye.

On the way home from the depot, we nearly had an accident. Still overcome with emotion, my mother had to hit the brakes on the '39 Chevy. This being many years prior to seat belts, I was standing in the backseat.

Clutching a *Grapette* soft drink in both hands, I had the mouth of the bottle in my mouth. (They stopped making that delectable beverage about 1950.) The quick application of the brakes sent me flying forward against the back of the front seat. The *Grapette* bottle jammed into my mouth, cutting my lips and gums.

At this point, my mother was really emotional. More like borderline hysterical, and with due cause. Her husband was headed off to war. She had nearly wrecked. Her precious three-year-old (me) had almost crammed a *Grapette* down his throat. A good case of hysteria was definitely in order.

Never mind that her reaction was understandable and warranted. At age three, I wasn't capable of logical reasoning. So, that's not the way it impacted me. My subconscious absorbed the feelings, and interpreted them very illogically.

Young children are exceptional observers because they're so sensitive to all feelings. However, due to limited cognitive skills, they're terrible interpreters. Thus, this experience was inaccurately interpreted by me.

As a three-year-old, it was an experience that etched a deep wound in my unconscious mind-- "goodbyes are grounds for hysteria."

As a result, for most of my childhood and adult life, goodbyes were terrible! I felt deep emotion. Would get teary-eyed over incidental goodbyes. Often resorted to wearing dark glasses to preserve my manhood!

At times, my emotional response to goodbyes was terribly embarrassing. It just wasn't cool to get emotional when the Lone Ranger yelled, "Hi Yoh, Silver" and rode off into the sunset.

For many years, I struggled with the *goodbye* problem. Finally, I did something about it. Got some good therapy. Healed at a deep level. Emptied a lot of *goodbye residue.*

I'm still not well from that bad goodbye, but I sure am better. Now, departures don't bring such intense feelings, and are much more manageable.

Are you afraid to be alone? Maybe terrified of rejection? Are you tormented by jealousy? Have trouble with goodbyes? Agonize with abandonment issues? Perhaps you're still clutching the pain from a bad goodbye.

Chapter 19

Boogie-Woogie
On
Beale Street

Married thirty-five years, Blanche and Barney came from Pennsylvania for joint intensive therapy. They would stay one week and do thirty hours in five days. In so doing, they would unpack the baggage from more than three decades of marital conflict. They had made it quite clear to each other, and to me, this was their last-ditch effort.   This would be their final attempt at saving a marriage that had produced three grown children and several grandchildren.

Barney was a high school history teacher who was quiet and reserved. He had (what I call) a *mid-line personality*. He was never very high, nor very low. As far as Barney was concerned, most of life was meant to be spent hovering close to mild boredom. That was the way he liked it.

Quite early in life, Barney had unconsciously adopted the play it safe maxim for living. His motto was, "Blessed are those who expect nothing from life; they shall not be disappointed."

Blanche was another story. She was animated, dramatic, and loud. As owner of her own real estate business, she trained new agents, and conducted seminars. She had (what I call) a *high/low personality*. Blanche was either up or down. She had never been bored in her life. By contrast, in early childhood, she had unconsciously chosen a different edict for living. Her motto was, "If you're disappointed, say so, and say it loud."

Blanche and Barney had been carrying out their *life scripts* with each other for thirty-five years. Understandably, that was the way they communicated for almost all of the first day of their intensive therapy.

In graphic detail, with words and body language, Blanche complained. She berated Barney with a long list of gripes. It was obvious she had said it all before-- many times.

Blanche said Barney never talked to her, wouldn't share his feelings. He read the paper too long, and never confronted his father. He wouldn't stand up for her, had been too lenient on the kids. Barney hadn't shown her enough appreciation, and was much too passive.

Blanche continued with her list. Barney wasn't active enough in church. Smoked too much, wouldn't eat the right foods, didn't take care of his health.

Furthermore, he didn't like to snuggle and cuddle. Didn't show enough interest in sex.

While trashing Barney, (for nearly five hours) Blanche cried, yelled, stomped, sobbed, criticized, and reprimanded her beloved helpmate.

Several times during that five-hour marathon, I tried to get Barney into the ring with Blanche. I asked how he felt? Would he like to say anything? Would he like to tell his side? Basically, he calmly and consistently declined.

Oh, he added a word here and there. Said

Blanche was "...mostly right, but maybe she exaggerated a little." But he never showed any emotion, nor verbally expressed a feeling. With only an hour left in the first day's session, Barney said he needed to smoke. Blanche rolled her eyes.

Before she could say anything, I intervened, "Let's take a five-minute break."

Then I cornered Barney and said, "The first day is nearly gone. You've driven a long way for this. So far, we haven't really heard from you. While you're smoking, think about using part of the remaining time to tell Blanche how you *really* feel."

When we reconvened, I said, "Barney would you like to start?"

Without answering me, he began moving up on the edge of his seat, and looking squarely at Blanche, he said: "Sweetie, do you really wanta know how I feel? Well, I'm gonna tell you. I'm sick of you! I don't like you! I hate being around you. I'm sick and tired of your complaining, bitching, and tirades. If I have to listen to you one more minute, I think I'm gonna throw up!"

Barney's bombshell lasted about five minutes. He was calm and stable. Thankfully, there was a trace of emotion in his voice.

Blanche went ballistic, squalling and wringing her hands. Said the trip for therapy had been a waste. Said she had the vapors, was about to faint, and needed someone to fan her. Said there was no hope. It was over.

"Blanche," I said, "I thought you wanted him to talk? Wanted him to stop being so passive? Wanted to hear his feelings?"

She said, "But I want to hear *good* feelings, not bad feelings!"

Lovingly, gently, and ruthlessly, I told her she couldn't have it both ways. If she wanted him to talk and share his feelings, she'd have to take the good with the bad. She didn't like it. But to her credit, she got a grip and listened.

At the end of Monday's session, I gave Barney an assignment. He was to write Blanche a letter telling her everything about his accumulated feelings.

Tuesday's session began with Barney reading his letter. It was ten pages long. It took quite a while for him to unload all the resentment he'd been packing around. When he finished dumping his trash, he shared some very warm and loving feelings, as well.

Blanche soaked up the warm fuzzies like a dry sponge. And she reciprocated with some affection of her own.

As the session was ending, I asked, "What did you enjoy doing together in the early days of your relationship?"

Simultaneously, they said, "We danced."

Smiling, I directed, "Then that's your homework for tonight. Go dancing."

That night, for the first time in many years, Blanche and Barney from Pennsylvania, went dancing in Memphis. They worked on the Texas Two-Step at a couple of country night spots, then Boogied-to-the-Blues on Beale Street.

There are a lot of different cliches about what keeps a marriage together. Most of them probably contain some element of truth. Here are a few examples.

"The couple that plays together, stays together." To be sure, having a common interest in recreation is an asset.

"If the bedroom is good, everything else will be, too." No doubt about it, a good sex life goes a long way in keeping a marriage healthy.

"Having children bonds a couple for life." Yes, I've heard many couples say they were staying together for the sake of the children.

"If you can work together, you can stay together." It's true. Couples that are able to work together in the same business are demonstrating a lot of staying power.

"The couple that prays together, stays together." Without question, having a mutual spiritual bond can be the glue that holds a marriage together.

The list of cliches offered as marital absolutes is endless.

Of course, none of these are true-- all of the time. Everyone can name couples who did some of the above and still split up. Some did all of the above, and still terminated.

Far be it from me to offer another marital absolute, adding to the infinite list of cliches. But I will offer an observation.

For nearly thirty years, I've worked in marital therapy. In that period of time, I have never known a couple to split-up who *regularly danced together*. Perhaps there are some, but I have never known or heard of them.

Dancing is about celebrating. It's about feeling. It's ancient, and it's current. It's about communicating, and it's effective.

Blanche and Barney from Pennsylvania worked hard during their intensive therapy. They dealt with a lot of issues. Their relationship *rebounded* and *rebonded.* They put the zing back in their marriage. Nothing they did was more important than when they started dancing.

God bless them.

Chapter 20

"I'm Not Very Good At Feeling Bad"

When she came for therapy, she was in bad shape. Severely depressed, terribly afraid, and very fragile. Habitually, when faced with such conditions, she had resorted to unhealthy compulsive habits.

She was determined to change the pattern. She worked hard, followed the program, and got better. Then she experienced a major relapse.

To explain her actions, she put it quite

succinctly: "I'm not very good at feeling bad."

She'd been doing great, and feeling much better about herself.   Then she was hit with a load of rejection, loneliness, and failure. She reverted to old habits. Normally, it's *the inability to manage the bad feelings of life that prompts destructive behavior.* Bad feelings, such as rejection, guilt, fear, loneliness.

Can you identify with not being very good at feeling bad? Admitting it could be the first step toward conquering it.

"How do I avoid setbacks?" It's a good question. I hear it frequently from those who've been in therapy. Usually it is prefaced with, "I feel much better. My life is healthier. But I'm afraid I'll revert to old habits? How do I prevent regressions?"

The key to success in avoiding relapses is to have *a plan to deal immediately with the bad feelings.* The old South Georgia proverb makes a good point. "When you're neck deep in alligators, it's too late to talk about draining the swamp."

Many years ago, I developed the following technique for handling bad feelings. This methodology has been quite helpful to me personally. Numerous clients have reported good results from memorizing and repeating this epigram. Hopefully, it will be helpful to you, as well.

***
THE FOUR A'S FOR HANDLING
BAD FEELINGS
***

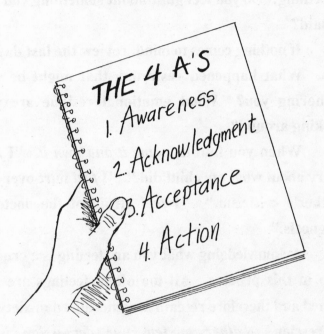

THE 4 A'S
1. Awareness
2. Acknowledgment
3. Acceptance
4. Action

AWARENESS. This is the self-sensitivity position. You're aware that something is wrong. You're slightly depressed. A little blue. Maybe you can't sit still. Feel a little anxious. Perhaps a sad news story or television program brings tears.

***

ACKNOWLEDGMENT. Having become aware that something is wrong, it's time to take inventory. What's going on in your life that you don't like?

What's happened in the past few hours that was upsetting?   Has   someone   hurt   your feelings?   Did you hurt someone?   Are you angry at something? Do you feel guilt about something you did or said?

If nothing comes to mind, review the last day or two. What happened yesterday that might be still bothering you?   What emotional residue are you packing around?

When you find it, *name it and own it.* "I *feel* angry about what my child did." "I *feel* hurt over my mother's criticism."   "I *feel* afraid of the doctor's diagnosis."

Acknowledging what you are feeling is a crucial step in this process. All too often, feelings are not named and therefore remain as generalized anxiety or depression. *Neither anxiety nor depression is a FEELING.* Both are symptoms of unresolved feelings. Unnamed and unclaimed feelings often surface as defused anxiety or depression.

***

ACCEPTANCE. Now that you've named your bad feeling, it's time to accept it. Rather than deny or discount it, accept it. "I know I shouldn't feel this way..." is a contradiction in terms. You either feel it or you don't. "Shouldn't feel..." this or that is irrelevant.

At this point, some people take issue with me. They often quote the Bible.

The Bible says, "If you have hate in your heart, you've committed murder already." They add (usually with gusto), "If you have lust in your heart, you've committed adultery." Then they ask, "How do you reconcile accepting your feelings with such strong biblical teachings? The Bible says some feelings are sinful!"

The answer is-- it doesn't matter. Even if you take these verses literally (which I don't), it still doesn't matter. *Believing a particular feeling is a sin, will not keep you from feeling it.* It will keep you from owning it, accepting it, or confessing it.

Denying you have a certain feeling, because you believe it is a sin, may make you hold it inside. Then it comes out as anxiety or depression and that will make you sick. That really is a sin!

Do not confuse *acceptance* with *approval.* Accepting your feelings is not synonymous with approving of them. It is perfectly healthy to say, "I wish I didn't feel this way. But I do feel this way. And I accept it, though I may not like it."

***

APPROPRIATE ACTION. Having named it and accepted it, what do you do with it-- this bad feeling? Choose an appropriate outlet. It is common to act on our feelings. In fact, the tendency is to go from awareness, which is the first step, to action, which is the last step. (That's what fills up bars for Happy Hour!)

How do you decide what's appropriate? That depends on who you are, your values, and standards. What's appropriate for one, may not be for another. I would not propose to tell you what is and is not appropriate for you. I will offer a few things, that in most cases, will be appropriate for everyone.

***

JOURNAL. Write down your feelings in a notebook, diary, or personal journal. Do not monitor what you write. Tell it all. Be honest with what you feel, even if it shocks you. This writing is for you and no one else. If you feel uncomfortable with what you have written, tear it up or burn it after you are finished.

***

EXERCISE. Do something vigorously physical with your bad feelings. Exercise with a purpose. The goal is to burn up some of your negative energy.

Release your anger on a punching bag or racquetball court. Or hit the bed with a tennis racquet.

Through running, walking, or doing an aerobics class, burn up your fear. Discharge your sadness, loneliness, or guilt through your sweat glands.

***

PRAY OR MEDITATE. Give your bad feelings to God, your Higher Power, the Spirit that is bigger than life. Get a mental picture that your negative feelings are leaving your body, mind, and soul. Let them dissipate into the hands of the Holy Other.

***

SHARE. With a trusted friend, spouse, counselor, priest, pastor, or growth group, share your feelings. Honestly and openly, tell someone.

***

MINISTER. Call or go visit someone who may be in a similar predicament. Don't talk about *your* feelings-- ask *how they're doing?* Listen empathically. Express your concern and support. Listening to someone else who is hurting can help put your own bad feelings into perspective.

***

THERAPY. If you are still having trouble with your bad feelings, make an appointment for therapy. Professional help can be extremely valuable in helping with your healing.

If you're not very good at feeling bad, try using the 4 A's:

Awareness

Acknowledgment

Acceptance

Appropriate Action

Memorize and repeat them regularly. These tools have kept many people from reverting to old destructive habits.

If you work the program, the program will work for you, too.

Chapter 21

"It Was Them Navel Oranges"

Willie Fred Wiggins was his name. Law enforcement was his game. He was the Barney Fife of South Georgia. He was a policeman who may have been more harmful than helpful. But he meant well.

Willie Fred was known for his law enforcement screw ups, his big heart, and his philosophical proverbs about life. He wasn't well-educated, but he was street smart. Two stories help to prove my point.

Willie Fred was in the hospital. I went to see him.   When I inquired about his condition, he responded, "Terrible upset stomach. Thought I was gonna die. Doc says it's a virus. But it ain't. It was them navel oranges."

"Navel oranges?" I questioned. The story continued.

"I went on duty last night at six o'clock. When I left the house, Evie Lou handed me a sack of six navel oranges. She knows I'm a fool about navel oranges. Me and Woodrow was on duty. First thing we did was drive down to the *Do Drop Inn* and eat supper. Woodrow had a chicken plate. I went for the catfish. Ate a big bait of catfish! With french fries and hush puppies."

"About nine o'clock, we was riding around checking on things, and I commenced to eat them oranges. They was fresh. Right from *Indian River Fruit Company*. Sweet and real juicy. Tried to get Woodrow to have one. Wouldn't take it. Said it'd give him heartburn. I kept eating 'em. Didn't pay no attention. Come eleven o'clock, I'd eat all six of 'em."

"Well, it was a quiet evening. Not much action. About midnight, Woodrow said, 'Willie Fred, let's get an ice cream.' I said, if you'll get 'em, I'll buy 'em."

"You know we're always cutting the fool about who's paying and who's not. Well, Woodrow said, 'Willie, you're on.'"

"He came back with a big triple dip of butter pecan. I ate every bite, including the cone."

The plot thickened, so to speak! Listening to the story, I kept a straight face. Don't ask me to explain how!

Willie Fred went on. "In about an hour, I began to have this terrible pain in my belly. Thought I was gonna die. Woodrow brought me right out to the emergency room. That's when Doc said I had a virus. But that wasn't it."

"The way I figure it, them navel oranges got all tangled up with the catfish, fries, and hush puppies. Then that ice cream kinda glued it altogether in a big wad. It just shut everything down and made a mess. I don't figure it was a virus."

"Neither do I, Willie Fred," I nodded, still keeping a straight face, (which I still can't explain!)

The second Willie Fred Wiggins story involved another mess.

A local, well-known drunk called Roy Bea had started a fight at the *Do Drop Inn*.

By the time Willie Fred arrived, Roy Bea had broken some windows and furniture. When Willie Fred tried to arrest him, he got resistant and started swinging a stick. Willie Fred was getting frustrated.

"Now see heah, Roy Bea, you've done made a mess and it's getting bigger. And see heah, the bigger the mess you make, the bigger the mess you gonna have to clean up!"

I liked Willie Fred. He had a way of getting to the point. Especially about messes.

In my work, I see a lot of people whose lives are in turmoil. Through inappropriate parenting, I watch parents damaging their children. I see teenagers engaging in self-destructive behavior. I observe marriage partners doing the same thing.

The morning newspaper and the evening news are filled with stories of people whose lives are haywire.

On occasions, I remember the redneck philosophy of Willie Fred Wiggins. Sometimes, I feel like saying:

"Now, see heah, you've already made a mess.
And the bigger mess you make, the bigger the
mess you're gonna have to clean up!"

Chapter 22

Wasted Worry

Worry is one of the greatest drains on human energy. Worry is the most widespread form of fear. It disrupts concentration, and interferes with sleep. Worry blocks productivity, and sabotages progress.

Few things intrude and impede peace of mind, like worry. Ironically, most of our worry is wasted over issues and concerns that never come to pass. All of us have heard the tongue-in-cheek proverb that says: "Don't Tell Me That Worrying Doesn't Help. The Things I Worry About Never Happen!"

An emotionally troubled teenage boy was taken to a therapist. He had a nervous habit of repeatedly waving his hand from side to side. The therapist asked him to explain his behavior.

He reported, "I'm scaring the snakes away."

The therapist questioned, "Do you really think you are scaring snakes away by waving your hand?"

The boy replied, "Yes, I am scaring all the snakes away."

The therapist responded, "But young man, there are no snakes in here."

Replied the boy emphatically, "See, I told you! See! See!"

My mother-in-law's sister was known as "Aunt T." A wonderful woman, she was a well-documented, card-carrying worrier. Once during a family crisis, my brother-in-law, Roy Reed, said, "I believe this is too much worry for us. We may need experienced, professional, reenforcement. Somebody needs to call Aunt T!"

My guess is, most families have a member who fits the same bill, and can identify with this story. Is there a chance you may be it?

Worry takes its toll on the whole person. Many physical ailments are closely related to worry.

Since every human being is conceived from a flawed genetic pool, we all have our biological weak links. Worry seems to aggravate and exacerbate these genetic weaknesses. Ulcers are irritated, not nearly so much from what you're eating, as *what's eating you*. Tension headaches may start from a genetic predisposition, but are often precipitated by fretting. People with facial or body tics are usually chronic worriers.

However, the physical problems not withstanding, the biggest price we pay for worry is emotional.

There is so much energy burned up in wasted worry! In its worst form, worry becomes obsessive, phobic, or manic, and is tormenting. More medication is prescribed for this problem (worry, anxiety, nervousness, obsession, mania, phobia) than any other disorder, medical or mental.

Worriers will find a reason to worry. Two stories illustrate the point.

The first one. Question. Do you know the difference in a psychotic and a neurotic? Answer. A psychotic says 2+2=5. A neurotic knows 2+2=4, but it worries him.

The second one. A neurotic is one who worries about acquiring a castle in the sky. A psychotic worries about living in it. And a psychotherapist worries about collecting the rent!

Confession. I've worried about collecting my share of rent from worriers.

In working with worriers, I've seen those who fret over the frivolous. Others have tics and nervous habits. Still others are tormented by obsessions, have phobias, and manic or panic attacks. I've seen some of them make great progress. Others very little.

From mild nervousness to the worst obsession, the common thread I have observed runs through all forms of worry. It's a consistent attitude about life-- Worriers take life too seriously.

Sometimes, they take themselves or others too seriously. Or they take achievement, education, or religion too seriously. Or power, prestige, or possessions too seriously. Worriers take life too seriously.

Some worriers are inclined to focus on the past. They lament all the bad things they've done, or not done. They can't forgive themselves and get on with life. Or they get locked in the *victim's role* and continually worry about how badly they were treated.

Others worry about the future. They seem to live by Murphy's Law: "If anything can go wrong, it will go wrong." They live with the dread and anxiety syndrome-- something terrible is always about to happen.

Whether the focus is on the past or the future, either direction destroys the present. Both are following the pitiful path chosen by all worriers-- taking life too seriously.

Connie had a double-dip of worry. She obsessed about the past, and all its tragedy. And she lived in constant fear of something terrible happening in the future. It was nearly impossible for Connie to converse in the present. All of her energy was drained in *lamenting the past and fearing the future.* There was no mystery as to why she suffered from chronic depression.

Many years ago, a long-term seminary president was well-known for his graduation day ritual. As the line would form to begin the processional, he would walk through the ranks, and mumble one statement over and over. "Don't Forget Rule 13. Don't Forget Rule 13."

By the time graduation day arrived, virtually every student under his tutelage knew about the wise old theologian's famous Rule 13.

His admonition for life was, "Don't Take Yourself and Life Too Damn Seriously."

I couldn't agree more. What a powerful piece of advice. Especially to a group of graduating seminarians! Or to anyone else, for that matter.

If those who make up the *worrying class*, could live by that counsel, what a difference it would make. What a great way to begin each day.

Today, I will not take myself and life too damn seriously.

Chapter 23

The Folly Of Fanaticism

We live in an age of exclusivity and fanaticism. Individuality, spontaneity, and creativity are frowned upon and often squashed early. Our educational, political, and religious systems are controlled by creeds rather than credos. *A creed is what you are taught. A credo is what you have learned.* Today, in our culture, credos are seldom tolerated.

All too often, schools, churches, professional institutes, lodges, civic associations, social clubs, prep schools, and universities want their people to look the same, sound the same, and act the same.

Unfortunately, when diversity is scorned and sameness is applauded, we end up with a tragic waste of human potential. The anonymous writer of the following piece was making just such a point.

***

THE FABLE OF THE ANIMAL SCHOOL

Once upon a time, the animals decided they must do something heroic to meet the problems of "a new world." So, they organized a school. They adopted an activity curriculum consisting of running, climbing, swimming, and flying. To make it easier to administer, all the animals took all the subjects.

The duck was excellent in swimming, better in fact than his instructor. He made passing grades in flying, but was very poor in running. Since he was slow in running, he had to stay after school. He also had to drop swimming to practice running. This was kept up until his web feet were badly worn, and he was only average in swimming. Since average was acceptable in school, nobody worried about that, except the duck.

The rabbit started at the top of the class in running, but had a nervous breakdown because of so much makeup work in swimming.

The squirrel was excellent in climbing.

But he became extremely frustrated in the flying class where his teacher made him start from the ground-up, instead of from the treetop down. He also developed charley horses from over-exertion and then got a C in climbing and a D in running.

The eagle was a problem child and was disciplined severely. In the climbing class, he beat all the others to the top of the tree, but insisted on using his own way to get there.

At the end of the year, an abnormal eel had the highest average and was valedictorian.

****

Our country was built on the principles of rugged individuality. The Declaration of Independence declares that all are, "...created equal and guaranteed the right of life, liberty, and the pursuit of happiness." Yet, the current atmosphere is often replete with extremism, exclusivity, and intolerance.

Carl Sandburg was once asked what he considered the most obscene word in the English language. Surprisingly, he replied, "Exclusive." I agree.

Exclusivity rejects those who think differently, believe differently, behave differently. Exclusivity takes a position of judging everything and everyone against a predetermined belief or standard of good or bad, right or wrong, correct or incorrect, normal or abnormal.

In religion, politics, and education, such views are rampant. *Exclusivity is arrogant and fanatical* and produces disharmony in our families, institutions, and country.

A large segment of current Christianity is militantly exclusive. This is, indeed, a rather bizarre thing. Bizarre because the Christian faith is built on the concept of agape-love which is all-inclusive and unconditional. At the core of the teachings of Jesus is, "Whosoever will may come." Arrogant religious zealots paraphrase this verse, "Whosoever believes AS I BELIEVE may come."

Hopefully, a new day will dawn when EXCLUSIVE will be viewed as an obscene word. How different the world would be if exclusivity was the only exclusion!

Chapter 24

The Accidental Tourist

Few things are more detrimental to life than lack of self-confidence. Feeling inferior, inadequate, and insignificant leave little room for confidence.

A man went for some psychotherapy to deal with his *inferiority complex*. After a few hours of testing, the therapist said, "I have good news and bad news. First, the good news. You'll be happy to hear, you do not have an inferiority complex. The bad news is, you're inferior!"

The beauty of this story is that it's true for everyone. We're all inferior to someone, and inadequate for some tasks. To own that is to claim our humanity.

Self-confidence is not reserved for the intellectually elite. It is available to everyone who acknowledges their weaknesses, and claims their strengths. The following story is about one such person.

When her husband left, Mary Rose had two preschool children. She went back to school and got a teaching credential. She raised her children alone. Both graduated from college.

Although she'd made it all work, she still felt terribly inadequate. In fact she had so little self-confidence, she was terrified of traveling by herself. In the first fifteen years after her divorce, she had never driven more than fifty miles from home.

When she decided to get into intensive therapy, she faced a big hurdle. It was five hundred miles to Memphis.

She asked about bringing someone with her? I strongly discouraged it. She had an urgent desire to get better, and her local therapist had recommended the intensive. So, with fear and trembling, she made the trip.

Mary Rose was a woman of incredible ability. She was talented in many areas. But she was paralyzed with her feelings of inadequacy. Her talents were basically dormant. With no self-confidence, she was like a flower that had never opened.

As a child, Mary Rose was victimized by harsh criticisms and neglect. In her early adult life, she was victimized by men. With such damaging residue, she had spent most of her life playing the role of the victim. Helpless, hopeless, and copeless. Results? No self-confidence.

When she got into therapy, she responded well to the maxim: *You're not responsible for being the way you are; but you're totally responsible for doing something about it.* She stopped being a victim. (None of us can prevent being victimized but we can stop playing the role of the victim!)

Mary Rose did some hard work in therapy, and followed through with unusual tenacity. A healthy self-confidence emerged. It changed her life in every way. Among the many changes, she was freed to travel alone, extensively. She loved it.

On her first big trip, she covered 3500 miles, and included Yellowstone Park and the Grand Canyon-- alone.

The day before she embarked on this venture,

she had a slight panic attack. She called me.

"I've got all my maps and tour books. I've studied them thoroughly. But I've just had a terrible thought. What if I get lost!?"

I responded, "You will get lost. There's no doubt about it. You will not make such a long trip without getting lost. *But you won't stay lost*! You'll take your map, find where you are, and get back on track."

She made the trip with minimal difficulty. Best of all, she loved it. Since then, she's flown to Europe three times-- alone.

However, traveling alone is not the biggest change in Mary Rose's life. As a result of the emergence of her self-confidence, her art work as shown incredible growth.

Mary Rose had taught high school art for many years. However, her low self esteem left her own artisic ability, tragically inactive.

Purging herself of the inner conflicts that had held her back, opened up a phenomenal artistic endowment.

What a talent! What a gift! She began to produce some extraordinary work. Won awards. Got plaudits. Wrote poetry. Got it published. And the beat goes on. Who knows what will come next.

Mary Rose is an exceptional person with a great story. She was nearly fifty when she *found herself*-- her soul-- her essence. It would be easy to get caught up in lamenting the many years she lost, due to a lack of self-confidence. To do so would be futile. Fearing the future kept her stuck. Regretting the past would do the same thing.

Mary Rose doesn't take the time to lament. She celebrates every day with self-confidence.

Chapter 25

Beginnings and Endings

Let me tell you about my grandson, Brady. He's the firstborn to our son, Matt, and daughter-in-law, Wende. In addition, he's the first grandchild on both sides of the family. To say the least, his birth was greatly anticipated by a lot of people. He didn't have a good beginning.

Brady was born nearly nine weeks premature. He weighed in at two pounds and nine ounces. Then he lost down to two pounds and three ounces. My wedding ring would go over his foot all the way to his knee.

His diaper was only three inches wide. You could see through his hands. If one of his ears got turned down, and he lay on it, it stuck to his head.

In neonatal intensive care, he was hooked up to tubes, wires, and all sorts of monitors. Sometimes he stopped breathing. Sometimes his heart would stop. The alarms would sound, and at first we would panic. Calmly, the nurses would walk over and shake the incubator, or thump him on the bottom and say, "Wake-up lazy bones!" And he would start breathing, and his heart would start beating.

After six weeks in neonatal intensive care, Brady went home. What a day! He had to wear a heart and breathing monitor for six months. All of us took infant CPR training. Thankfully, we never had to use it.

At fourteen months, he weighed twenty-five pounds, had four teeth, and began walking. Brady had a very bad beginning with a very good ending.

Life itself is a continuum of beginnings and endings-- endings and beginnings. There are sunrises and sunsets, and introductions and conclusions. Doors open and close.

Seasons begin and end. Careers start and finish. The school year has a beginning and ending. Children stop being children. Years come and go. There is birth, and there is death.

Life is never static. It's always changing, and it does so, mostly, through repeated beginnings and endings. Nearly everything has a beginning and an ending; except church!

Several years ago, when I was still trying to be a pastor, I made a pastoral visit. Went to visit a man who never came to church. At one time, he had been a very active churchman.

During our conversation, I said, "Earl, why don't you come to church?"

He replied, "I finished."

Rather startled, I responded, "Excuse me? You finished?"

"Yeah. I used to go, but I got done. Some people go to church one, two, three times a week, for years. They don't ever get through. But I did. I went to school and finished. Went to the army and finished. Then I went to church and finished that, too."

Most things have beginnings and endings-- for Earl, including church.

I heard Robert Fulghum say: "All any of us really want out of life is a few good endings."

I think he's right. In marriage; with our children; in our careers; regarding our parents; with our health; in our faith; and with death. All we really want is a few good endings.

After listening to people for nearly thirty years, I've drawn a few conclusions regarding endings.

***

1. *Only you can make your own good ending.*

All too often, we depend on someone else for good endings. Down in South Georgia, they say, "Every tub's gotta sit on its own bottom." In case you need an interpreter, that means-- you, and you alone, can make your own good ending.

***

2. *You cannot be responsible for someone else's good ending.*

Those with a high guilt complex spend much energy trying to make someone else have a good ending. It never works.

***

3. *What we tell ourselves is the key to an ending being good or bad.*

Self-talk is the key in defining how we assess good or bad endings.

***

4.   *It's never too late to turn a bad ending into a good ending.*

Much of life's misery comes from holding on to bad endings. The choice is yours. Maybe it's time to turn that bad ending into something good.

***

This chapter began with the story of my grandson, Brady's, premature birth. Fortunately, his bad beginning had a very good ending. I'd like to close this piece, and <u>Heroes of the Heart</u> with a letter that I wrote to him on the day he came home from the hospital.

****

November 11, 1993

Brady Matthew Doyle
1355 Silky Cove
Memphis, TN 38134

My dear little Brady,

Today is a very big day in your life. You will not remember this experience. Many of us will never forget it. In fact, there are many such experiences already under your young belt. Memories that you will not recall, but for us they are cut indelibly on our minds and hearts, forever. And, of course, that's the way it should be.

Oh, you may carry some *primal memory residue* from these first few days of your life, but probably not very much. Certainly, not enough to worry about.

Besides, with the abundance of attention, affection, and assurance you're going to receive, I suspect you will actually benefit from these early experiences, rather than being negatively impacted by them.

But wait a minute, I've rambled on much too long. That's a trait of mine, that you, like the others, will learn to tolerate. What is the significance of this day? Why all the fuss about November 11, 1993? It's your *homecoming*-- your graduation from NICU (Neonatal Intensive Care Unit). This is your official *Welcome to the Family Day.*

In some strange way, it feels more like your "real" birthday. Believe me, Brady, the 11th of November will be remembered by us as much as September 28.

Who knows, you may even have two birthday celebrations every year. Wouldn't that be a treat.

Brady, to fully understand this, I need to get philosophical for a moment (another habit you'll learn to tolerate). A wise man once said, *All any of us really need from life is a few good endings.* I agree.

Some things start well and end badly; others start badly and also end that way. But having a few things in life that end well, just makes all the difference in the world.

Take you for instance. You started out on a pretty sour note, little Bubba. I'm talking really sour.

Your preparation for entrance to this world was going just fine. As far as we knew, your mom was having a picture-perfect pregnancy. The morning yucks had been short and she was carefully watching her diet. She was exercising regularly, and doing everything possible to give you every advantage in your prebirth state.

Your dad was doing an admirable job, too. He touched you and talked to you through your mom's tummy. And as I understand, even periodically had some private father-to-son chats.

What I'm saying is everything was going just great, as far as we knew, until September 27. Your mom went in for a regular checkup. And because they were going to do an ultrasound test, she carried quite a crowd-- your dad, Grandma Martha, and Aunt Leanne.

Through the miracles of modern medicine, each of them wanted to get an early peep at you. It never happened. After the routine tests were done, it was apparent that everything that had seemed so right was now terribly wrong. And in the next few hours, it got much worse. It got so bad both you and your mom were critically ill. At that point, it seemed that a great beginning was getting very close to a horrible ending.

Gratefully, that terrible ending was averted, and we were all wonderfully relieved.

You were taken from your mom surgically, which means they opened her up and took you out. You were not nearly *done.* You had only been developing for thirty-one weeks. That's not good.

You were extracted from your warm-water bath to be thrust into a world of tubes, needles, strange noises, and machinery. You didn't like it. And you looked terrible.

What a radical turn of events for us all. One day, the future and everything in it looked bright and exciting. The next day everything looked bleak and empty. To say the least, it was not a good beginning.

With your mom still very sick and you being quite critical, your dad had his plate full. For several days, he balanced his time between supporting your mom, and keeping a vigil by your incubator. He touched you, talked to you, prayed for you, and cheered you on. He bonded with you (two months before your due date) in a way few fathers have the chance, or the inclination to do.

You know what? Neither of you will ever be the same because of it. You will have a relationship that has a mystical closeness. Both of you will know it, but neither of you will be able to explain it.

On with the story.

With lots of great medical attention, modern technology and expertise, plus family support and prayers, you did remarkably well-- growing, developing, and gaining weight. And today on this special day, you are up to a strapping four pounds and nine ounces. Wow!

Brady, over the years, I've known hundreds of families and couples. And I want you to know that your mom and dad have one of the best young marriages that I have ever seen. They are really good for each other and to each other and they have an abundance of love to share.

So, in spite of a very bad beginning, as the son of Matt and Wende Doyle, you are a very lucky little boy. It is already evident, that in spite of all the problems, they are really good with you. No doubt, they will provide an environment where you can grow up to be what you were designed and destined to become.

Maybe I should tell you a little more about your parents, starting with your mom.

It's been nearly six years since I first met your mother. From the very beginning, I liked her a lot. I mean, I liked her a lot!

Over that period of years, there's never been a time when I've questioned my original judgment. She is intelligent, disciplined, well-balanced, and emotionally stable.

Your mom has good practical sense, is warm, loving, and really easy to be with. She even tolerates our neurotic interest in sports,

And excessive family togetherness. She is very special. I am really proud to have her as a daughter-in-law, and she is going to be an outstanding mother to you.

Your dad? Well, I've known him since before he knew himself. Waiting at the hospital, on the day you were born, brought back memories of the day he was born.

Unlike you, your dad was about two weeks late. Apparently, he wasn't eager to leave his cozy little comfort zone. We went to the hospital three times trying to coax him out. Twice, he refused. I've often said your dad was born in 1964 on July 25, 26, 27!

Your dad came into this world comfortable and really laid back. The first time I saw him was an hour after he was born. (In those days, fathers weren't allowed in the delivery room-- pretty stupid, huh?) He was lying on his back in an incubator. His hands were behind his head, and his left foot was propped up on his right knee. He's a trip, Brady.

Your dad is a rare combination of the tender/tough man. He's sensitive and emotional, but handles crises with calmness and assurance. He doesn't panic easy, maybe never. He's at his best when things are at their worst.

Your father is going to be an outstanding dad to you. My greatest hope is that he will be as proud of you as I am of him.

So, little Bocephus, the first six weeks of your entrance into this world was a very poor beginning. But as of today, that ordeal has come to a very good ending. And we celebrate that good ending by welcoming you to our world. Have a good journey.

With much love,

Papa Don

11/11/93

TO BE CONTINUED

The Going Sane Series

The Going Sane Series is a three-volume set. <u>Heroes of the Heart</u> is the first book in the series.

Volume two will be released in the fall of 1996, with volume three following in the fall of 1997.

To order additional copies of <u>Heroes of the Heart</u>, use the order form on the back of this page.

ORDER FORM

To order additional copies of *Heroes of the Heart*, do one of the following:

1. **Fax Orders:**   901/751-4140

2. **Telephone Orders:** 901/751-4140

3. **Mail Orders:**   **Asa HOUSE Books**
   P.O. Box 381604
   Memphis, TN 38183-1604

4. **Please send____ copies to:**

Name: _____

Address: _____

City, State, Zip:_____

Phone: (____)_____

5. **Charges: $17.95 per copy. Add $3.00 for packing and postage. Each additional book, add 75 cents. All Tennessee addresses, add 8.25% sales tax.**

6. **Payment:**

   __ **Check**

   __ **Money Order**

   __ **Visa__ MasterCard**

   Card number:_____

   Exp. Date: ____/____